Author of the Book

Ali Hurd

All rights reserved. No part of this publication may be reproduced, stored in a retrieval system or transmitted in any form or by any means, electronic, mechanical, photocopying, recording or other- wise without the prior permission of the publisher or in accordance with the provisions of the Copyright, Designs and Patents Act 1988 or under the terms of any license permitting limited copying issued by the Copyright Licensing Agency.

Published by: KPT

Cover Design by: Brynda Goldsmith

A CIP record for this book is available from the Library of Congress Cataloging-in-Publication Data

ISBN-10: 9798336719499

ISBN-13: : 978 X XXXXX XXX X

Distributed by: Amazon

ALI HURD

Somerset Paranormal Tales

Breaking the Illusion

Dedications

In loving memory of our beautiful Kathleen.

To Toni & Jonathan Tiffany and Kathleen' grandchildren.

To my three girls Lauren, Ella and Tayla and my grandson Jensen.

My amazing, supportive partner Mark and my best friend Helen Murphy

Chelsey-Anne, Ricci, and Evangeline-Rose

Callum, Alfie, and Ella

Poppy and Charlie Maicee-Jo, Jacob, and Eryn

Josh and Charlotte

To my amazing and beautiful designer Bryn

Disclaimer

We at Somerset Paranormal Tales do not and would never claim to be medical professionals. If you require help with your medication, please seek help from your GP or other medical professional.
Thank you.

Somerset Paranormal Tales

ALI HURD

Somerset Paranormal Tales has always prided itself on love, light, and positivity! This is not just a book about the paranormal, it is a journey of Self-discovery, adventure, and excitement. Break through your ego and fear and start truly living life.

Every reality exists right now. You do not have to create it; you have to access it. That's one of the greatest tools that there is when it comes to true ascension, it will change what you are capable of. It will change your awareness, actions, and perception. It will change your life from beginning to end. These capabilities have always been inside of you, you've just never had anyone to guide you, or to teach you to tap into that part of yourself!

There is a whole side to you, that you have not met yet! Unleash it.

We are all born as spiritual beings, but that side of us becomes dormant over the years by things in our food, water, medicine and even the air we breathe. Our whole belief systems are completely programmed wrong, so we never discover the power we hold inside of us.

This book could change your entire future! You need to read it with a very open mind, keep pausing, think for yourself and remember, we have broken through our egos, so everything in this book comes from a place of compassion and love. It's not meant to cast criticism, insult or judgement. This book will not be for everyone, it requires you to set aside your ego and really think about the message. If you're reading this and think anything negative is aimed at you, sadly your ego is too dominant, and this book will not change that. This will only help those who truly want to break through the darkness that surrounds us all. That makes you feel like you are drowning, until you break through and see the world how we do, in all it's beauty! See how incredible you can become and really start to live. Wake up to the real reality, not the illusion you have been sold.

But it also requires you to put the work and effort in, to achieve this. This book is purely for guidance and real-life experiences. The rest is up to you.

We are a team like no other! We do not have egos that need feeding. We are not here for popularity, likes or fame! We genuinely want the world to be a better place, and to see people living and enjoying every moment of this human experience! It's a whole new level of freedom that you will not believe until you achieve it! Please read this carefully, digest the information and actually think!

As I have used real life examples, I have no shame, and these things were told to me at different times in my life, so if it's someone I know and you think it's about you, you have some work to do on yourself, because I speak of truth, not a fake truth. We just don't sugar coat anything, we are real and honest.

This book will only resonate with those who really want to turn their life around and finally be happy and rid of everything that holds you back, that stops you from moving forward. As a team we are constantly moving forward, helping each other grow, encouraging each other, celebrating each other when we reach new levels, we don't compete against each other, because only people with big egos treat life like a competition.

Or people who keep up false pretenses because they feel people would not approve of them if they did not pretend to have the whole fancy lifestyle, completely happy and content with life.

The world does have to change, but not the way those in charge want it to, so we have to at least try to make a difference with all the knowledge we've learnt and been taught by incredible people, I'm glad my path crossed with a certain white witch, because it's through her brilliant teachings that I've been able to then teach the team.

We are all here ready to help or answer any questions, we like helping and guiding people, we even see our supporters growing and opening up, it's pretty incredible to witness. Because every single one of us was born with a gift, it's whether you are brave enough to let go of your ego to discover your natural gift. People spend hundreds on seeing psychic mediums, when you're probably capable of contacting them yourself if you follow our process to break through your ego.

CHAPTER ONE

Let's start by talking about what being an empath is. A true empath is a highly sensitive person who has so much empathy that they take on the pain and emotions of others. Any tragedy or disaster, an empath will absorb all the emotions and sometimes it can be very overwhelming. I didn't know I was an Empath until someone with knowledge started to guide me, I had spent years thinking that something was wrong with me, thinking I had mental health issues when all I really needed was guidance. During my darkest times, I shut myself off from the world for several years and found I could not cope in crowds due to the bombardment of emotions. The overwhelming feelings that purely took my breath away with no explanation. I was confused and anxious, so of course in comes the anxiety medication, then side effects from that, moved onto something else, then another issue suddenly pops up. Medication after medication truly stopping me from accepting myself. This is another reason for this book, because so many people don't know who they are or are lacking acceptance.

So many wander around feeling that they don't belong, don't fit in and left with zero confidence because they have never been guided by that which we can't see, like compassion, it's a feeling right? You feel it. But you can't see it can you? But you know it's there because that's what we've been taught to believe!

Empaths are amazing people, true hearted empaths are rare, these are people that literally would move heaven and earth for someone they love, true empaths, they feel such strong deep love, and are extremely sensitive, has anyone ever kept telling you, you are far to sensitive? It is so invalidating to feel like you're wrong for feeling the way you do when you cannot help it.

Moon cycles affect empaths, especially true hearted ones, we have certainly learnt that as a team, the highs are absolutely amazing! But there are low times too, it's like a roller coaster. We have been following and logging moon cycles for a very long time and having a team going through the same highs and lows is what gets us through, there are also other ways to cope with the lows, which I will explain in another chapter.

Some people go through life feeling like something is missing, usually empaths, so they can become addicted to things because you're trying to make up for what you feel is missing, chasing highs which ultimately leads to addiction, it makes you feel good or even numb for a few minutes, but then you're back and your head is wanting another high, these in our opinion and our research are usually empaths. We are not medical professionals, but from experience, some people diagnosed with mental health problems, a lot are unguided Empaths, the signs are like mental health symptoms, but no pill is going to help an Empath, so hopefully this will help you off the medication.

Signs of being an Empath

Do you over think things too much? Like really over think to the point where you are focused on the worst outcome.

Do you get paranoid very easily, especially around certain people?

Are you to emotional or labeled as "Too sensitive" by friends & family?

If someone you love is distraught, do you start feeling it?

Do you get overwhelmed in crowds? And when you get home do you feel emotionally or mentally drained? Do you need some alone time to recover?

Do things easily bother you, like excessive talking, or smells and noises?

Do you try to get out of going to events? Not because you want to, but because you know it will drain you, sometimes for a couple of days!

Do you overeat or under eat due to emotional stress?

Are you afraid of becoming consumed by intimate relationships?

Are you afraid to trust people because you've always been let down or disappointed?

Do you feel you can't be yourself?

Do you constantly worry about things that have not even happened?

Do you feel you don't fit in or belong?

Do you feel you have a purpose, but don't know what it is? Do the smallest things make you extremely emotional?
Do you go out of your way to make someone else happy, even when you feel broken inside yourself?

Do you give relationships your all, and never receive the same love & respect back?

If you answered most of those with a yes, the chances are you are in fact an empath. This book will unlock that part if you are. There are great benefit's of having an empath as a friend, they are great listeners. They consider your emotions and truly care about your well-being. They are loyal and trusting! They appreciate everything about life. They do not get consumed by the materialistic world. They love the outdoors and sunsets, but more so the moon. They only want the best for you. They bring out your passion. They make your life so much brighter! Discovering and embracing the empath side of you can feel so empowering, but not in the ego sense, it's a whole new amazing feeling!

But sometimes it can be a curse. True empaths are prone to attracting dark empaths, these are the complete opposite to true empaths, they want praise, popularity, constantly crave attention, chaos, and drama, they will literally fool you blind. They are master manipulators, and I've had my share of encounters with dark empaths, it's the worst kind of betrayal, you let them into your heart, you give them your trust, and all the time they are in a constant state of reaching for more.

When you discover you are an empath, your whole perspective on life changes, you realize that trust and love are honors that shouldn't be broken! I've had many secrets confided in me, secrets that stay with me even if that person does not. I deal with the hurt and move forward, I don't live my life to please others or to fit 'a box'. I would rather stand alone than be untrue to the person I know I am. I never had any self respect until I discovered my empath side and fully embraced it. Some people might think I love myself, and yes for once in my life I do love the person I am now and I got this far with help from two people and all my research, I didn't pay for courses or hire life coaches, I learnt all this side myself and I want to help others find out who they are, that's the only goal here. Because if I can do it, then so can you!

But we do now know the signs of dark empaths, being an empath and feeling hurt is difficult, you literally can't breathe.

I lost two people I cared about, one person meant a lot to me, and I couldn't go to the funerals, I had to say goodbye in my own way. I grieved silently because my feelings were invalidated and the pain I felt for the families was all too consuming, I felt numb for them. It's okay to grieve for people you once loved, it was part of your human experience, part of your story, so your feelings do matter! You shouldn't have to hide and deal with it alone.

My team are the most supportive, selfless people I've met! They don't run when I'm low. Before I worked through everything, I begged my team to let me go, I thought they were better off without me, I thought I was toxic, but they wouldn't let me go. They cry with me, they listen, they consider my feelings, me being happy means everything to them and I didn't except or realize that until February this year. So, we talk and then we shake it off and have a good laugh, we support each other with everything, even little things! So, for us now, being an empath is great and incredible when you find your people!

Learning to ground yourself and protect your energy is a must in our eyes, there are a great range of meditations on grounding. But mine, I usually get up, put my hand on my heart, breathe in through my nose and out through the mouth, feel the silence between beats, focus, then imagine stepping into a gigantic disco ball, feel the shine, the sparkle, the light, let it flood down through your head down into your arms and down through your body, all while breathing and focusing. It's normal to feel tingling, sometimes a little lightheaded, but it will keep you grounded and protected!

Also as an empath, it's important to take note of your moods between moon cycles, you should find a pattern eventually which will better prepare you for the lows, but once you have embraced that side, the right people will come along and you will build amazing new friendships. It is pretty amazing and absolutely priceless! It may open your eyes to current relationships and friendships, and re-evaluate their value, but why hold on to people who stop you from moving forward and growing? Does it make sense to cling to people who don't wish the real best for you, who don't encourage or support your dreams?

It's okay to walk away from people. One of the hardest things you have to go through as an empath, is grieving for people who are still alive! I've heard many accounts from people who don't know they are an empath, and they are struggling with family, mostly their kids' birthdays being forgotten, yet their family members best mates' kids, get taken to concerts or special things done, so they struggle trying to tell their children it's not their fault. I'm not giving details or digging, but I removed my children from something because nobody spoke to them, their anxiety got too much, so we just left and I won't ever put my children through that again, I don't care who you are! Being an empath and feeling their emotion was heartbreaking, but it also gave me the strength to stand up for them and protect them. My children are not perfect, but they have faced many battles that others know nothing about and if people don't want to know them, then it's their loss not my children's. Because they all have absolutely incredible hearts.

When an Empath taps into their power, it's like Neo waking up in the Matrix, it's the only thing we can really relate it to, in a way that would help you better understand. Empaths penetrate beyond masks, feeling the importance of the soul, sensing intentions, sensing wounds. Feeling the emotions of others, feeling their pain or a happy moment in their life, sometimes these feelings can make you overwhelmed, to the point you yourself cry. Empaths decode the essence of your whole being, and once they embrace and step into this whole new awareness. They are forever changed, it's literally like a switch has been flipped and there is definitely no turning it off!

Chapter Two

As we are born as spiritual beings, we all have our own unique vibration/frequency...We don't talk science or anything like that, this is all about that what we can't see!

So, everyone and everything has it's own vibration/frequency this is shown in our moods, especially in Empaths, some people go through life thinking that people always leave, but sometimes it's not you. Until I learnt and researched, I thought there was something wrong with me, people always left with no reason, just gone, but when you understand vibration/frequency it makes sense! So, when you feel really good and you make an effort with yourself, your vibration is high, then the next minute you feel down, depressed, and alone, just lost in complete darkness this means your vibration/ frequency is fluctuating, like an emotional rollercoaster. Compare it to 'fussy eaters,' one minute you love something and then you go off it. Because even food has it's own frequency/vibration. It's why we are drawn to certain things because it matches our vibration, colours, styles etc., and if it doesn't match yours, you go off it and that's the same with people, some people just leave because you are on a much higher vibration/ frequency than them, so you no longer resonate with each other.

It does not mean you are any better than them, it just means your vibration/frequency doesn't match up, people can grow overnight, you can sometimes tap into your higher self without knowing it.

So, I want to explain a little about chakras, because the colours and crystals have their own unique frequency and vibration.

The human body is actually a community of different frequencies, there is a map of the human body that has existed for thousands of years. It

Breaks the Human body down to seven major energy centers called chakras. Each chakra is associated with a different part of the body. Each chakra is also associated with a different colour based on the frequency that part of the body operates on. Your body is a map of colour, colour affects your emotions and your thoughts. It can even tell you what foods are necessary at a specific point in time to rebalance yourself physically and energetically.

Additionally, when we refer to food, we are referring to natural food that has not been created or altered by man. Food is your medicine and colour is your guide.

Red (Root) - Vibrates at the same frequency of emotions, such as hunger, anger, stress, and aggression.

It is the most important chakra to keep balanced because it's foundation of all your higher chakras on the physical realm, red corresponds to your hips and specifically your legs, which connect your body to earth. It is the colour that connects you closer to the physical realm rather than the spiritual realm. It is a grounding colour. An imbalance of your red chakra can cause bowel disorders, urinary problems, and many other muscular issues associated with the hips & legs. If you are experiencing such issues, simply eat foods that are red: Tomatoes, strawberries, and red apples etc., by surrounding yourself and consuming the frequencies of earth matter that correlate to the red frequency and rebalance your imbalance.

Orange (Sacral) - Vibrate at the same frequency of feelings such as creativity, ambition, sexual energy, and addictive behavior.

It is a colour filled with passion and emotional expressions. On the physical realm, orange corresponds to the reproductive organs, if you are experiencing a lack of sexual energy, start surrounding yourself with orange frequencies. Eat carrots and oranges. These foods will surely rebalance your sexual energy to a healthy state.

Yellow (Solar Plexus) - Vibrates at the same frequency of emotions such as positivity, power, inspiration, and intelligence. On the physical realm, yellow corresponds to the spleen and the stomach. It relates directly to digestion. If you suffer from depression or even poor digestion, start spending more time outside in the yellow sun. Eat a mango, banana, or pineapple. You will soon see that your depression will dissipate as you inherit healthy forms of the yellow frequency from the natural world.

Green (Heart) - Vibrates at the same frequency of feelings such as love, compassion, healing and giving.

On the physical level, green corresponds to your heart and lungs. If you are going through heartbreak, surround yourself with green. Walk around a luscious garden. Eat a kiwi or green apple. Embrace and inherit a balanced green frequency.

Blue (Throat) - Vibrates at the same frequency of feelings such as communication, truth, and balance.

On the physical realm, blue corresponds to your throat and your Thyroid. If you experience trouble expressing yourself, spend more time sitting by the sea (preferably a blue one). Eat blueberries, visualize a clear blue sky in your mind's eye, and allow the healthy frequencies of blue to rebalance your system.

Indigo (Third Eye) - Vibrates at the same frequency of feelings such as, deep thought, intuition, and sensitivity.

On the physical realm indigo corresponds to the pituitary gland. If you are trying to focus to attain a higher level of intuition, eat indigo foods, such as blackberries or plums. Visualize the colour in your mind's eye and see how it affects you.

Violet (Crown) - Vibrates at the same frequency of feeling such a high spiritual attainment and self-actualisation. On the physical realm, violet corresponds to the pineal gland. If you are in search of attaining a higher level of spirituality, consume foods such as beets and figs. Doing so will allow you to inherit the highest frequencies in the right spectrum of vibration.

You can use the colour of food as guidance on what to consume, it's hard to begin with, because of all the foods we have become addicted to, that really are not good for us, there is something in these foods that cause the addiction. The shape of food is equally as important, because the shape of food is a good indicator of what part of the body it can heal.

For example, a carrot is good for the eyes, and it kind of looks like an eye when you bite into it.

Walnuts have always reminded me of tiny brains, and walnuts are good for the brain.

Now you have a little more awareness of the right kind of foods, that will not only benefit your body, but it will also aid in your development. But it is having the willpower to not go back to the foods that don't serve you, they just poison you slowly.

There is so much information available about the body and the affects food has on it, the more you look into it the more aware you will become, and the days of visiting the doctor will be way less, opinions change, frequencies do NOT!

So always remember that food, good food, holds it's own unique vibrational frequency.

Sometimes the ego can be blamed, well most people do think you have an ego problem, it's easier to label than to understand what we can't see. It's how we have been taught, it's programmed into our belief systems, and we are thrown science and other distraction tactics because that's what they are! So, a scenario is, you have been friends with someone for years, they know everything about you, and they suddenly leave you with no reason or goodbye! This is because people with ego radiate to 'damaged people' that's what they are labeled as, damaged. People who judge others, love drama and chaos, and live with their ego, prey on those they think are weaker, to feed this ego.

If you have a friendship like this, know you are not weak! You are only human, and when you no longer are 'damaged,' and you need them less, they disappear with no reasoning or a goodbye!

This is not a reflection on you. You are just now resonating on a much higher frequency than them (are stronger), so they just leave. It's so sad, it used to cripple me when people just stopped bothering with me, with no word, but empaths know when someone is like this, we get feelings in the pit of our stomach. I always ignored these pit's because I didn't know what it meant. I now understand. I don't have any ill feelings towards anyone who does this. Honestly, they helped me grow by leaving. Those who stick around for and through everything, are in your corner celebrating! And understanding this, has lifted so much fog from my mind.

So, when you come across someone and you just think, 'I don't know you, but there is something that I'm unsure of', it's nothing wrong with them, please stop judging, unless you have good reasoning to!

People have to stop this judgement on others! It's just a person who doesn't match your vibration/Frequency that's all, they could be the loveliest person to others resonating on that same vibration, just not yours!

When you start this journey of self-discovery, and you start to connect and break through the ego, you will notice your vibration/frequency rise. It's like a tingling warmth start from the head down to your feet, it feels amazing and freeing, I love it when my vibration rises, I literally bask in the warmth, it's a whole new feeling I've never felt before in my life, the team love the feeling too.

When you understand about vibration/ frequency, it's easier to keep your vibration high, you find ways to lift it, mine is usually chatting to the tea or popping on my headphones with my favourite music and literally dancing it out. Writing this part of the book, we have just come through the eclipse season, which was tough on the team, but we all came through because we had each other to lean on and know you're not going bonkers. Most people wouldn't have a clue what I was talking about, so when you do embrace the empath side of you, you will find people you are drawn to, and new friendships will be built. You will resonate so much more with people the same as you.

Frequency and vibration is how I was taught to read spirit's, it takes focus, but when you get cheeky spirit's who left this life on your frequency/vibration, and they come and wind you up, it's funny! Spirit's have a sense of humour like they did on this plane.

Everything is energy and everyone is energy! With it's own unique frequency/ vibration, that's how you get items with attachments, because whatever it was, your frequency/ vibration has imprinted onto that item, it's residual energy, all your data stored in something that can't be hacked, including furniture, your memories, your life forever imprinted on your things! People who absolutely love nature will resonate most with what I'm explaining, because nature has it's unique vibration/ Frequency it's pretty beautiful. It's like when you touch someone and give them a little electric shock, that's a true spark, connection, your vibration/ frequency is a big match in our experience! Next time you take a walk, pick up a leaf, really study it, see it's veins, it's life force, then cup it in your hand, close your eyes, focus on your breathing & your heartbeat, listen to the silence between beats and you will feel that tiny vibration from that leaf (this may not happen straight away) it is incredible! You can also do this by placing both palms on a tree, you feel the life force, the energy, when people say go hug a tree, you really should try it and focus when you do.

People should spend more time in nature, especially if your mental health is a little off, with empaths, being out in it or by the sea, it's great therapy, actually look around and study what
a beautiful thing the world really is, we don't appreciate all that we have, because we are constantly being distracted by the latest technology, it's such a shame that we have been so heavily manipulated by rich powerful people, we have been completely used and abused!

Find you, fall in love with your own heart, set yourself boundaries, it's not selfish to protect your vibration/Frequency, it's self-respect, as long as you don't turn bitter and nasty, you will be winning at your life experience! Understanding that when you are in the best of moods, that's where and how high your vibration/frequency should be, so it's just learning the balance.

At the moment it's a depressed cycle or something else? while it may seem you're moving through molasses and that you're caught in between worlds, that's the energy balancing taking effect. With an active sun, pulsing higher frequency through our solar system, it takes time to assimilate the higher frequency light, which is literally changing the way you think and act.

There are so many nighttime meditations on YouTube that can help you with your frequency/vibration, I'm just explaining in short terms without the technical stuff! That's hopefully the goal here, we talk in easy talk, so you best understand what we are trying to say.

Most of us on the team use Jason Stephenson, he has a fantastic range of guided meditations on YouTube. He has a really calming voice. Experiment and find what resonates with you and your frequency, you may find you resonate with sound ones and not guided.

Everything in life is about what resonates with you, don't be afraid to just be you, life can be pretty draining when you're trying to be someone you're not, all through fear of being judged or spoken about, what can words actually do to you? If you worry what others think all the time, or if you are just trying to fit in and be accepted, it's not really living is it? Why would you want to spend your human experience on earth trying your hardest to just be accepted? Why do you spend energy on making others happy through fear of rejection? It's not living, is it?

Laugh more, stop worrying over silly things that are not important. I know sometimes it can feel like the most important thing on the planet, but it really isn't. What's really important is your happiness and joy levels. If you have low joy levels, you will only attract the lowest forms of joy. I expect there are some of you who don't have an inch of joy. But that's not true, because the joy is there, deep inside of you, it's at a low level because you haven't ever connected that part. Yes, things give you joy for a minute or two, but it doesn't last. Imagine feeling joy and happy all the time, and it's the same with everything else, when you start focusing on the things that bring you joy & happiness, your frequency skyrockets, your love you hold in your heart, it takes on a whole new level and feeling.

There are two sides to everything that exists. Find your other side and you won't look back. I choose to laugh more at things in life and I let stress go now! I take good care of myself; I am happy within my whole core. I want others to feel the same. That's our drive. So that's a little on vibration/frequency, I'm better explaining it in person or on live anyway.

CHAPTER THREE

My story

WARNING! THIS COULD BE TRIGGERING FOR WOMEN WHO HAVE EXPERIENCED THE LOSS OF A CHILD! SO PLEASE SKIP IF YOU ARE EASILY TRIGGERED

This chapter is to share my experiences. Your traumas, they matter and so do your feelings. I understand all to well.

As we go through life, we have so many different emotions and circumstances hit us, some completely knock the wind out of us, but it's knowing how to control your emotions and focus them in the right direction!

When we lose someone, we loved or once loved (well in truth that love will always stay with that version of you). But we look at someone passing differently. Yes, we grieve for that person, and that big empty hole that's left behind where that person used to be. But they are not gone, our belief, our experience, and our data, tells us they never left us.

We just can't see them, but they watch over us and give us little signs. We see it as they graduated from this life experience. We are here to learn.

Maybe people are taken before their time in our eyes, but really, they learnt the lesson they were supposed to in this life, you wouldn't want to hold anyone back you love right? When you truly love and care for someone, you do want to see them succeed and reach their highest potential? well we all do anyway, so as much as the pain literally cripples you, you have to look for the bigger picture and find a positive as painful as it is!

Watching an illness take a loved one is extremely hard, I think that is the hardest one, how cruel it is to live your last weeks in pain. I do feel for people who have to sit and watch someone you love so much just fade away, that kind of grief never goes away I don't think, but again, they wouldn't want you to not live, so live life for all of you.

I carried the pain of losing my son through my whole life, until I connected with him in Nov 23 it was a feeling I can't describe, I went numb, but that ache in my heart, it isn't bad now, I know who he is with and they are happy. So, I keep that in my heart, happiness is all that matters. Like me, and I'm not telling this for sympathy or attention, No ego remember! I'm trying to show that I am a flesh & bone person with real feelings! And I really understand grief, so I'm telling my story to show you that I understand, and to hopefully teach others to start caring the way they should, about people they claim to love.

At 17 years old I fell pregnant. It was a shock at first, but I did everything right. I stopped smoking and started eating healthier. As each day passed, I watched my bump grow, I sang to it, I would catch the foot or hand, whatever poked out first. I had created a life for me and my child in my head. Most people have great memories of turning 18 years old, but I don't, when I turned 18 I still had my son alive inside me. I remember it like yesterday, the movements just stopped, so my mum took me to the doctors, and a heartbeat couldn't be found.

I was sent for an emergency scan, it was a young girl who did the scan, and she just got off the stool & ran out, I had no clue what was happening, it was a couple minutes before the door opened again, and when it did a man walked in followed by the girl wiping tears from her cheeks, and I was told my baby had died, the next hour was a blur driving to the hospital, because I was so far along I was induced the contractions started slowly, it had been a few hours and I got off the bed to go over to put something in the bin and my waters broke, the contractions started getting stronger, I became distressed, so they pumped me full of drugs, and after 10+ hours it was time to push, and I was so broken into pieces, knowing I would never be walking out with my baby, the last push felt like forever, I remember saying "I can't, I don't want to" but I had to, and I did and I was told it was a boy, they gave me something else which sent me to sleep, I woke the next morning, and I was just so broken, a nurse came in and asked if I wanted to see him, and I said yes, I took in every single feature on his little face, and she said sadly he had got the cord tangled around his neck & feet, there was nothing I could of done, I was young and still heavily medicated, so my mum made the choice for the hospital to arrange a cremation, going home to baby stuff was so hard, packing it all up, returning the pram and other items. I had a photo of him which I stupidly kept in my purse, and my purse got stolen one night at a karaoke night, I took the microphone and begged for whoever had taken it to take the money, just leave my purse where it would be found, and sadly it wasn't left or found, and it broke me, because that's all I had. And I know I'm not the only person who has experienced this sadly, so it will resonate with a lot of ladies, it's not meant to hurt anyone or cause pain, it's okay to feel how you feel, it's okay to grieve for what could of been, it's okay to feel sad every year, every birthday they are not here to celebrate, it's okay to hurt And this is what I mean about judging people,

You have no idea of what they have been through, the battles and trauma they have suffered. So, I'm saying it's okay to always love & remember, we need to be able to talk about these things, people really don't understand others struggles, but we do! And then he was forgotten by everyone except me and someone else. I had to deal silently alone, and I guess that's where my compassion comes from, because sadly I've experienced some awful traumas, but I know now that I wouldn't be who I am today if I hadn't experienced these things! And yes I did go off the rails, there was someone I knew of, who was pregnant the same time as me, they drank and did drugs and had a healthy baby, how was that right when I had done everything I could to make sure my baby was healthy? So yes, I really lost it! And I have more than paid for my mistakes, some people don't let you forget the bad bit's about you, they don't believe you can change, they don't look at what caused you to make mistakes!

This has never been more true for us!

Love doesn't hurt us! People pleasing hurts us! Pretending everything is okay hurts us!
Silencing ourselves, hurts us! Having no boundaries hurts us! Not having our own backs hurts us! Self-abandonment hurts us!
Another person's unhealed traumas, hurts us!

Love liberates, and rational challenges shine a light on where we are not yet liberated!

We are human beings, we should be connecting and enjoying life, but again our biggest weakness is used against us, FEAR!

Life has become a competition for a lot of people. The desire to have a fancy home, flash car and fat bank accounts comes first. You work every god given hour just to keep up this lifestyle. Before you know it, life is over and what have you done?

What have you really achieved, the time you miss out on spending with those you love most? Are material things worth missing out on? Like building memories, with loved ones, children, show them how to live, how to love, don't teach them that material things are more important than those precious things, those precious moments, I don't understand sportsmen who would rather kick a ball or hit a ball, than go to that precious family event, after all, when one dies, you wish you had more time for that person right? So why are you not making the most of being around the people you claim to love, making the effort to show them that they do matter? And mostly that they are not alone.

They were never wrong when they used to say, "Money is the root of all evil". Look at how much you actually spend on top of the range technology, it's ridiculous! All for a brand, a name, I don't let money rule me anymore, I did once, but then I discovered what life is truly about, it's making memories and having that human connection which we have lost!

Nobody wants you to live how we live and see life. This is something I always look at and say to myself... I will breathe.
I will think of solutions.

I will not let worry control me. I will
not let fear control me.
I will not let my stress levels break me.

I will simply breathe, and it will be okay because I don't quit! Not until my time here is done.
It is incredibly hard to speak the truth, when people don't realize they are living a lie!

But I always talk from the heart, and I never fake my care for people, if I stop bothering physically with you it's because I found out you were not worth it or you were abusing it, but I never stop caring! This heart has grown tired of constantly hurting! I know so many people feel this way but are frightened to just be themselves!

We have been manipulated in so many ways, and we are taught to believe in a lot of things we can't see, but when it comes to the spirit world, people don't believe? Yet we teach our kids, as we were taught, to believe in the Easter Bunny, Tooth Fairy, Father Christmas and even the devil, but not the light, the positive spirit realm or realms that exist, that we can't see.

I have studied the paranormal for 31 years now, I made sure I did my homework properly! I didn't just think "I'm going to buy equipment and be a ghost hunter" there is so much more to it than that. You have to be able to know exactly what you are doing in our opinion, because it's not a joke! So many people have come to us for help, and we are tired of cleaning up other's mistakes, so we just do us, I no longer take on others' problems as my own like I used to, I got used and betrayed quite badly! We turn down agents and agency's daily! I didn't start this for fame, popularity, or money! I just want to learn and understand, nobody will ever own Somerset Paranormal Tales.

We will always stay just us, searching for the truth, trying to understand and ease people's fear of death! It shouldn't be feared, live your best possible life with no fear, what will be will be!

And when I talk about the ego, it's like people who have a dream, they want to be something, but they don't want to give up their lifestyle. They want others to pay for that dream, how is that right? To us it's pretty selfish, you have top of the range technology and cars, yet you expect everyone else to donate their money for you to achieve your dream?

I'm living my dream, and I've asked no one for money to be able me to live my dream. I just made sacrifices here and there, cutbacks, I do not make any money out of what I do! I do not want to be the best; my ego was shredded a long time ago! And it takes a lot of work to change your mindset and belief system, it doesn't happen overnight, you have to look at yourself and ask yourself what you truly want from this life experience, everyone has a passion for something! But again, it's stupid things like grammar, that winds me up! If you can read what it means, why does it matter if it's missing an exclamation mark or a capital letter, it's crazy! But that's how we have all been programmed, well not all of us!

I've always thought outside the box, and if something doesn't make sense, I have to research and make sense of it. I spoke out a lot at one point in 2020 I was hurled abuse and labeled a conspiracy theorist, but everything I spoke out about was true, so how was I a conspiracy theorist? I cared about people and wanted to protect them, and I wouldn't go back and do anything differently if I had the chance, because I would rather stand alone than live in a fake world, full of people just existing...But people don't understand because their Ego and the programming gets in the way, and what I researched I didn't ever want to be right, I wanted to be wrong, but I wasn't wrong, and I had nightmares for month's, my compassion for humanity is off the scale! And there is someone very special to me who I would like to thank for never letting me down, for always being there when I was hopeless, someone who didn't abandon me, but taught me strength and to never doubt my truth, someone who woke me up to the real world and set me on my path of researching the truth, and that's my beautiful friend Michelle West, a very beautiful soul indeed, and who I'm proud to call my friend xx

Also my very best friend Helen, who listened to me, looked at my research and who now thanks me for waking her up, so do a few others who listened to what I was saying, my Helen has seen me through some very dark times, again no judgement, just love and support, over 10+ years of solid friendship, someone who I know would never abandon me, even if we don't agree on something, she's always been there for me, she knows everything there is to know about me, and who I know, absolutely loves seeing this version of me, she's incredibly proud of the person I've become, and she's glad she stuck by me and watched me grow into this person, she loves who I've become and so do I xx

But people whose egos got dented, they wanted to be right, they were right, yet they had done zero research, just heard the paid expert's and their words were the truth, when sadly they

were the enemy! And looking at my life now, there are people missing who I thought would be here forever and I know why, and it absolutely breaks my heart. I beat myself up quite badly, thinking I hadn't shouted loud enough, but then someone taught me that sadly I can't save everyone like I wish I could, it's impossible, and I know they are helping me on the other side as we call it.

So, in order to change your life and create a brilliant happy future, you have to be willing to face your fear! You have to break through your ego, it's not weakness, it's strength, and breaking through your ego will cost you your old life and friendships, but the end result is beyond amazing! You will read real accounts from the team in the last chapter.

You have to really look at yourself in the mirror, keep telling yourself you love YOU, until you start to believe in yourself and believe you are worth so much more than you think!

I did it through so many tears, the emotions, guilt, shame, anger, every emotion, and everything you don't like about yourself, you have to start loving who you are, it doesn't matter what you look like, it's just a shell. We are not given an instruction book on life, don't be ashamed of mistakes you made, did you learn from them? Yes, so stop beating yourself up, it's not your fault, don't be ashamed of your scars, the heart & soul inside of you, it's what counts, it's what makes you - you. You shouldn't dislike anything about yourself.

Self love is one of the greatest lessons to learn, it's empowering when you are content and comfortable with who you are, but not in the "your better than anyone else" it's a completely different feeling! And we want more people to experience and find who you truly are, stop letting influencers with great bodies and good looking faces flash in your mind, it's an illusion, life is an illusion, and to break the illusion you have to break through the Ego and materialistic world, because it's not real, the people are real, but they are just selling you something that's all, the world is a stage; do you think they really care about you?

One of my biggest shocks on TikTok being our main platform, is seeing people do these battles for gifts, like what? You are chucking gifts at someone because they are good looking? Your money is going to someone who does not give a single thought about you after they have taken your money, some even scream for people to send a very expensive gift, and people do it for a glimpse of recognition? It's just bizarre, do they support you if you go live? No, they say they will drop you a follow if you subscribe, like that is going to change your life, it's just insanity! I like to personally respond to my supporters, and I do genuinely care about our community we have built, I don't ask for subscribers, and I do not beg for gifts! We have hundreds of silent watchers, and I hope they are learning from us, I do not sit there repeating "Tap that screen until your fingers fall off every 10 minutes, and share the live" I don't ask this ever, because I'm there to share our journey not to be on a leader board, it's insane how social media has manipulated the minds of people, and I am not picking on anyone, I'm just stating facts! Social media has been turned into a weapon of destruction of your humanity! How can people not see this?

It's the same with funerals, people crying over the deceased person, and you didn't bother with them when they were alive? You had the chance to be in this person's life, you left them, now you're crying over old memories, it makes no sense at all?

I had two funerals I couldn't attend; one was because I respected the family, I can't change my past and I shouldn't be judged through others' opinions or trouble making, how is that fair? So I grieved silently again, and it's hard, really damn hard, again my feelings didn't matter, I had to "Not think of the past" this person was important to me once, I cared deeply for them once, and it was complicated, but we always remained friends and I absolutely loved seeing them happy, it's all I ever wanted for them! How does that make me a bad person? Enjoying seeing someone you once cared deeply for, enjoying their life and being happy in love with their soul mate?? I have since spoken with a family member from one funeral, and they helped me see it was okay for me to grieve, it was okay for me to feel, and I hope I helped them too, or gave them some comfort.

I don't want people to feel sorry for me, I'm not sorry for me! It's part of my life experience and I have every right to talk about my life to help others! I look at it as, I wasted so many years on people and things that didn't matter, no matter what I did, I was still not good enough, and then I woke up, so I'm telling my story because if I can stop someone else wasting their years on the wrong things and wrong people, well it was worth me losing and wasting my year's, so I'm okay with that.

The best way is to write it all down, what you don't like about yourself, and look at each thing, it won't be because you don't like these things, it will be because someone else made you feel bad about these things. Write your emotions down, really think hard, and work through each one.

I will talk about emotions and how to break them down, and what questions you should ask yourself.

Anger, shame, guilt, every emotion, but this last one is key, FEAR.

F ace
E verything
A nd
R ise

That's what it's all about, facing everything!

You have to ask yourself difficult questions, like why do you really want to lose weight for instance? Are you doing it for yourself? Or are you doing it because that's how bad people make you feel? How does society make you feel? Because I bet it's not for yourself really, and that's the sad thing, that people are doing things and acting a certain way because of how society has made you feel and think.

You should be comfortable and be accepted for who you are inside, not how you look outside, it's your heart that makes you beautiful, your soul.

So, when looking at yourself, you have to look at everything and every emotion, and I will tell you now, only those who really want to be happy and content with life will achieve what we have.

I'm an ex-alcoholic, 18 years sober now, am I ashamed of what I was? Absolutely not, I was but not anymore, nobody knows what drove me to that, nobody wants to take responsibility for not supporting me, so it's easier to just label me and be ashamed of me, rather than sitting me down and asking what is going on, being a support network, they just left me to deal alone as I've done with nearly everything in my life, but despite feeling let down by the people who I thought loved me, I was the first one to offer my support, my ear & shoulder when things happened to them. But that's who I am, I will never turn anyone away, because I know what it's like to feel you have no one.

Those people don't know this version of me, they never stuck around to see me finally find my path and work through my difficulties so it's their loss now. I'm definitely not the same person I was five years ago, a year ago or even 6 months ago. I am always growing and learning. I'm proud of who I have become, and proud of how many people I have helped to finally feel they belong and fit in this world.

Money doesn't rule me or own me like it once did. It's actually surprising how money can change a person, bring out their greed, their ugliness, money truly is the root of all evil. Money takes over emotion.

I'm not here for popularity and I am a creator and person who isn't afraid to say things how they are, even if it hurts egos. It's not intentional, I just can't be fake. I won't lower my frequency or vibration just to match other's. I will never ever be untrue to myself again.

This is my life story, my human experience, so I will tell my truth always. I don't set out to hurt anyone, but if you ask me something, I'm not going to say what you want to hear. I am sometimes a bit brutally honest, but I am always me.

We will continue on our journey loving every moment we can. I won't lower my boundaries for just anyone, anymore.

Give it a try, you can change if you want it bad enough. If you want to stop hiding away, stop feeling rubbish about yourself, then you have to put the effort in. Nobody is going to save you. You have to save yourself from yourself and that takes some strength, which is what we try to give people.

Drop the fear and face your fear head on. We are live every night if you need a little help.

CHAPTER FOUR

The first step you have to take is to identify exactly what you want from your life experience, there has to be something deep inside you that you have always wanted to do or be? Write a list and narrow it down to the top four, use those as your focus. Search deep inside of You! Whatever approach you take to this, the most important thing of all is to know exactly what you want and give it as much clarity as you possibly can.

Focus on the feelings of love inside of you. Everyone has a deep love and deep affection for something, and it's just waiting to be unleashed. When you zoom in on love, instead of negativity, it will bring you great things. Don't be afraid to dig past the surface of your frustration and lose love or friendship in that area of your life. Love is never forceful, and it will never make you do just anything, it is your choice who you open your heart up to and who you don't. Know which hand to shake and which hand to hold. Those are key points too! Hesitation kills and the what if's, drain you. Don't devalue yourself or hesitate to do something, go for it, be bold, be brave. It's not going to be without flaws, because that's how true growth happens, you learn from those flaws, don't call them mistakes, get out of that frame of mind. Remember everything is a lesson!

We are taught to believe in God, and other beings and we do without seeing them with our own eyes, we just believe, but how trustworthy were the people who wrote about the past? We never met the people, we just believed their words, and everything we were told about, us, history, heaven, because it's logical explanations right? But is it really? What actually is logical in a spiritual world? Things happen that have no explanation for, until someone is paid to create an explanation that can be seen in words or pictures to sound logical. I hope you understand what I'm trying to say? We do not know the truth because the truth has been hidden behind false illusions, why do we worry about the past? It's gone, you can't go back, so let it go.

Was it okay for humans to be slaughtered for their spiritual beliefs? Their lives taken at the hands of someone else's orders, I wouldn't intentionally murder another human for their beliefs or anything for any amount of money, it shouldn't even be a thing.

As I've said, we are never taught anything about what we can't see, you see all these paranormal programs and said most haunted locations in the world, but not everywhere has been investigated, so how can you claim that? I don't claim to have the most haunted shed in the UK or world, but many in my position with an Ego would, they would be straight to the media with stuff we have captured, I don't make a big deal out of it, I clip it and chuck it up, people make of it what they do, they are entitled to their opinions on what they see, if people think it's fake or staged, that's up to them, we know the truth and that's good enough for us!

People quote the bible; despite the fact it was rewritten 100 years ago! It was purposely changed to hide things from us and to cause division. People are quoting the bible now, saying "look the Bible, it told us this was coming" no it's rubbish, they like to show us how they are manipulating our minds, but there are minds like ours that can't be manipulated, it's had so much FEAR added to it, and why? do you ask?

Because we are all hamsters running the wheel of wealth for those in charge, they get rich off of us being sick and ill, and doing everything they tell you to, tax the hell out of us, while they live in luxury and do whatever they like, Is that fair? Please sit back and re-read that, forget your tv and really think about it! Does that sound like people who care? The people that will commit hideous crimes against humanity for money and status is shocking! You can buy scientists for £10,000 or more, to manipulate the science to fit their agendas, and people sit back oblivious to this fact!

Like me a so called conspiracy theorist, who stated things in 2020 and got hammered for it, yet what I was warning people about then came out as true, Facebook would highlight my posts by independent fact checkers, who are people sat at home and in THEIR OPINION it's misinformation, these independent people who do zero research on what your saying are allowed to mark it as misinformation, just on their opinion, how is that right?? That's like you coming up to me saying "I broke my leg" and me just looking at you saying, "well in my opinion you haven't" and you would say, "But I've seen a doctor, been to hospital and had a scan & I'm in plaster" but I still say "in my opinion you haven't", it would be very frustrating right?? Now apply that to me trying to warn you about something, or tell you something is coming, I've done all the research, I've looked at all the statistics, which didn't match up either, and all you have done is listen to the media, it's hardly fair is it?? Especially when people know me so well and know I would not state something without evidence!

We are expected to work until we literally die, there is no retiring like the rich, we have to work our butts off so they can hide money in off shore accounts, invest in new treatments before they actually come out, you really do need to wake up and break through into reality!

Yes, it's scary at first, but not if you already have people who are awake to the awful things being done to us, chemicals and genetically modified things in our food, it's killing us slowly! When are you going to realize the real power is in the hands of the people, but again FEAR holds people back from doing anything! You have to dissolve your ego if humanity is to stay free.

Because the rich won't be having bank accounts monitored or themselves will they. So, because we don't have money or status, should we be treated differently? I don't understand people who pay stupid money for a brand that's been pushed by someone famous, just for a name?? Like your paying £100 for a zip-up jacket just because it's branded, have a think, there are people in the world that could do a lot more with that £100 it's insanity. Over £1,000 for a phone, as long as you can text and ring, does the make or brand really matter?? You're literally letting thieves rob you blind, right in front your face.

I don't ever want to be a part of the fake materialistic world ever again! Not that I raised my kids on brands anyway, but if you think about it, bullying happens to kids who can't have branded things, so your actually assisting in bullying by spoiling your children with top of the range phones and clothes, sorry but I want my children to be able to wear what they like and have a phone and things not branded, without feeling they will be bullied for it.

I see people constantly moaning about the younger generation, but we as adults fell into the technology trap, which we then allowed into the minds of our children, you have to look at yourself, there is so much in life that you don't see, because you are drowning in keeping up with other's, I would rather stand alone than go back to the fake materialistic world, the illusion!

I treat spirit's as if they are people, with respect, I don't demand or command things, I simply ask, just because I can't see them doesn't mean I have the right to hurl abuse or treat them like performing monkey's.

Imagine being stuck, and you need help, but none can see or hear you, then someone comes along, and you can communicate, and you think finally someone knows I'm here, then you communicate, and they just leave, it's not very fair, is it? To build hopes up and because you can't see them, they don't matter as long as you get what you want, it's wrong in our opinion, which is why I took the time to learn and be taught by a brilliant woman to cross spirit's over.

I won't abuse the spirit world just to get what I want, we do not work like that, and I'm sorry if I upset other paranormal people, it's the truth, you should learn to help them.

People think we are just another team out to make it big, well that couldn't be further from the truth, because we will always choose love & happiness over status and money!

We do not operate like any other team of researchers or investigators, we operate completely differently, but again it's gone off others' opinions and judgement. But we won't change to become popular.

There is a lot in the world we don't see, we don't notice, but when you take a step back and really open your eyes, look around you and others, really look hard. Open your senses, because once those senses are open, you feel the people you have lost around you all the time, you feel their energy, their love, we all have spirit guides, except those who sold their soul for fame.

Yes, there are satanic cults around, right under your nose, some you look up to, idolise even, they do many rituals and other horrific things.

Evil does exist, but not in the way it's been programmed into our belief systems, again that's done to keep you in fear, you have to look into what we can't see, because it is there.

It is like a thin curtain between worlds, not everyone comes back or through, again we believe you leave on what frequency you were resonating on, so if you left life on a high frequency you have no need to come back, you achieved everything and learnt what you needed to, yes they check in on loved ones, but they don't make contact, we all meet up in the end.

I don't like people who pray on others desperation to hear from a loved one, it's so easy to read a scenario, it will fit you somewhere, and I've been to fortune tellers, one was good, but it took me doing this to want to know and hear exactly what I needed to.

Some fortune tellers who get a good reputation end up ruining themselves by greed, money again! I heard of someone with a good reputation and I went to see them, was very good but within a few months their price was doubled, and it's such a shame, if I could control who comes through, I couldn't charge people, your giving someone something really special so that should be enough, your drive, not making people pay double because you got popular.

So, I can tell you with all our data and information that yes the spirit realm, world, plane, whatever you want to call it, yes it does exist! And it's not demons you're talking to pretending to be your relative's, that bugs me so much. Understand what you are looking into, connect yourself back to your dormant side, it will help you in your research so much more.

A team I watch in America, I noticed were getting personal connections but they didn't know it, and they wouldn't take advice from me. Why? because the Ego again. Why shouldn't we be helping and exchanging information? It's not because I'm not well known, but if I were, they would be straight in touch and that's the reality of it.

I did try reaching out to one of them and they just laughed and said I was funny. Well sorry but if they were to reach out to me now, I would tell them to jog on and that they are funny. I was quite disappointed to find out they actually have a gigantic Ego, so no, I wouldn't want to work with them now and I've stopped watching them. I noticed they got a little out there more and I did mention them in my first book, so who knows, if I did help get them some subscribers. I'm more disappointed that they aren't really the people they portray on their YouTube videos. We are happy to just do us, it's much easier and no complications, which is what we love, uncomplicated lives.

You really need a good, strong spiritual connection to counterbalance everything, you can't see it, but it is there!

We have the opportunity to face the dark, and all that we hide about us ourselves, and become something pretty incredible and empowering once we are through it. As I said, I have no fear, not even writing this, if I upset certain people, it's not deliberate, it's how it hit's your Ego. I get to tell our truth, our awakening and how I have broken through the illusion.

CHAPTER 9

Working on yourself and everything about yourself, is the best investment you will ever make.

Through shifting your thoughts and feelings, and looking at things from different perspectives, it really can have such a positive outcome in your life, you won't instantly go for the negative reasons in a situation or decision.

Now this is a technique taught by Mel Robbins, a life coach and motivational speaker, he released a science backed study, where you wake up and go straight to a mirror, you look hard and the reflection staring back, with no judgement or dislike, you focus, set an intention of what kind of day you would like to have, and then high five yourself, it may seem absolutely ridiculous, you may feel silly even, but you will eventually let go of those feelings, it does work, I've done it myself many many times, it's called the law of attraction, I don't teach that, but there are some incredible people who can, and I'm sure there are books on this subject.

Also another exercise that can work and help, is each day you wake, go to the mirror, again look hard at the person staring back, tell yourself that you love you, and that you forgive yourself for any mistakes you may of made, again the first few times can feel silly, but if you do this consistently, eventually you will start to believe in yourself and that will help you massively in dissolving your ego.

Changing your mindset takes strength, and you won't achieve it if you just rush through it, you really have to think about everything and write it down! That's really important, because you don't know who you might meet and be able to help, that's what life should be about, helping, supporting and loving each other instead of competing, because I bet you there is someone in your circle of friends that you are envious of? Maybe they have a better house and lifestyle that you crave, but are these people truly happy and at peace with who they are? Absolutely not! They may look like the perfect family on social media, but in reality it's not perfect, if you live in the materialistic world, you will never be truly happy and you will always feel something is missing and live your life envious of other's, does that sound like a well lived human experience?

Choosing to live your life at peace and loving the person you are, surrounding yourself with people who care about your emotions, who you can call and they would happily just listen to you break, no words, just listen and be there for you, and then when your finished, they turn around and say "I've got you, we will face this together, you are not alone" That right there could save a life!

I see so many people post about always pick up the phone, message me, but when you do that, they just say, "Oh sorry to hear that, maybe you should talk to your doctor." They don't really care at all; they post for likes and to make themselves look and feel good. Actions speak far louder than words, and that was all I needed to know about that friend. It's the biggest knock back ever, thinking someone loves you because they claim to, and then they don't really want to know when you're in a bad place, they don't really care about your feelings or emotions. Non of this matters to them. It is soul destroying finding out you gave your heart, and they pretended to. It breaks you and you feel even more alone than you did before you reached out.

I understand why so many can't cope with life, because in reality nobody does care. People are too wrapped up in competing and being envious of others or people pleasing. Is getting a hundred likes on a Facebook post worth someone's mental state? or even life? Because it really shouldn't be.

I would happily sit and listen to someone I love or care about breaking down. I would do everything to help them get back up. I'm not here to be liked or to live as a fake person. This is what I show my whole team. I show them what love and life is truly about. I will sit for hours with any of them and let them express their feelings to me. This also goes for my family.

I do my best to try to get you to be comfortable with who you are, dress how you want to dress, be who you want to be. As long as you feel good in your outfit that's all that matters. Why are others always seeking others approval, I don't understand it?

I wear what I like, I have my hair how I like, and mostly I act with nothing but a genuine heart. It all depends who you are, and what you want from me. I never act with unkindness and never have bad intentions towards anyone.

Sadly, people have used me to gain things. I've been the best thing when I'm giving, but when I can't do a favour, I then become the bad guy, when what do you actually do for me? Do you visit or check up on me? Do you sit and let me break? Because if you are one of those people then I will be loyal until the end, and I will do anything and everything for you, because what I have always expected from others, well it doesn't cost you anything!

All I've ever asked is for love, respect loyalty, that doesn't make me a bad person to expect those things, does it? But if you're ashamed of me or feel embarrassed for others to know we are friends, then you can say goodbye, it's that simple now! Because no way am I ever going back to changing me to be liked or constantly seeking others approval, I've simply stopped caring

about that, I care about my own well-being for once in my life! I won't tell you what you want to hear if you ask my opinion on life, because I don't live in that world anymore, and everything I do have strong opinions on I have spent months & years researching, I wouldn't just spout something without facts!

But again, society has been so heavily programmed, it's not until you step out the illusion that you see it, so much knowledge about us has been hidden, about who and what we really are, that's why there is always a distraction chucked out there, to divert your eyes from the truth!

Every single one of us comes into this world as a spiritual being, we hold huge light inside of us, power in our subconscious, and when you connect back with that side of you, you do see the world for the beautiful thing it really is, everything we have ever needed in cures has always been in nature, it's been right in front of us, but again big pharmaceutical companies came along, so the natural cures were covered up for example did you know that:

Dandelions: They are not just garden weeds, but they can stimulate the appetite and help massively with digestion, they have antioxidant properties within them.

They can help the immune system, help in detoxing your liver & gallbladder, as well as help with kidney function. Why are we not taught about this wonderful weed and it's capabilities??

Why are doctors giving you toxic rubbish when it's right there in nature and doesn't contain toxins that aid in your pineal gland being calcified (Pineal gland is also known as your third eye) Ask any herbalist about the benefit's of dandelions, they will tell you the same!

That's just one thing, there are so many more, I've cut right down and I'm weening off all pharmaceutical products, not everyone can do this obviously, because sadly the damage done by toxins from pharmaceuticals, stuff in our food, water and air, it's too far gone, that's without the damage that radiation has done to us on top. We are just Guinea pigs & money machines to the rich and we always will be unless we bring about change, bring the experts through with the knowledge of natural things for health issues, I know of someone who extended their life by 8 1/2 years when given just 3 months to live, she refused all treatments and went to nature, and nature brought her the gift of walking her daughter down the isle, seeing her grandchildren born (yes I've had permission from the daughter to tell this) I can't tell you exactly how she done it, but if she had tried treatment it wouldn't work, and she told me something inside of her screamed no chemo or radiotherapy, because you will be gone in 2 months, so she researched and tried everything! And it wasn't cancer that sadly took her.

All this knowledge is slowly being erased because people like me are speaking up, we are trying to open eyes to what the world really is and how it's run by evil. Because before long it will be too late sadly.

I mean what could they actually do to us if we were all United and stood up to them for once?

There are way more of us than them, it's FEAR that stops many, so break through it.

We are human spiritual beings, which means there will always be challenges and changes that hit us, there is no way of stopping those. We all learn ways of dealing with these in our lives, these challenges and changes can affect your vibration, which is the low mood you feel, don't be fearful, just face them with open eyes, have a think, look at situations from different sides, not the one side you are always presented with by someone, feel deep within you because the answers are always there.

Meditation at night, and if you have never done meditation, don't worry about it, it took me months to get into it, I kept at it I didn't give up after a couple of weeks, and it's okay to fall asleep to it, even asleep it's still reconnecting your brain, or rewiring it as we say!

You will definitely know when it's taking effect, you will notice different things about yourself, like something that usually would have upset you, but you just brushed it off and continued. Or you might have thought you were cold hearted, and suddenly things will matter deeply to you, that wouldn't have mattered to you before, you wouldn't have cared but it will matter.

You don't have to put everything on social media, just to make it look like you are happy and loving life, why fake anything?

You have to keep going with the meditation and thinking like we have explained, Because it will be working even if your asleep, most of us on the team do 8 hour ones, but we are all pretty good at it now, we are actually doing a team test, just to see what happens, and if we are successful it could be really good for us.

Just sit or lie down, chuck your headphones on, relax, get really comfortable, and switch off from the world, as said previously go to YouTube and look up Jason Stephenson.

So, while you are working on yourself, meditation and getting out in nature is a must, look at the world and really see it, it's pretty incredible. And another little secret, we don't even take up three quarters of the world, a lot of the world is hidden from us too!

During my research I came across the most incredible places, untouched by man, just beautiful stunning places, again the stuff is slowly being scrubbed from the internet, but I made notes on everything!

The world could be a truly incredible place, if people break through their egos, and see what's right and wrong, as stated. I'm not here to upset you, it's just trying to get you to see that what your living is a fake reality, meeting strangers on the internet who again, mostly don't care about you or your feelings, it's all about what they can get and the popularity, not your feelings, they stand up for you to make themselves look like heroes, when really they are no better than the person or people who upset you, your giving them that ego boost they need of being popular, and why are people so frightened of someone you have never met in your life? Why won't you stand up for yourself? You have a voice, stop being a door mat or someone else's ego boost, be you, be real, you don't need to follow the crowd to be happy and content, following the crowd only brings misery, and back stabbers, just be your authentic self, the truly incredible human you are, and were born to be, you do not need status of money to be happy, get it out your head.

What's meant for you will be for you, and what isn't meant for you will take itself out believe me! Deceitful people will always come unstuck at some point, you never have to dress up the truth, so don't go giving your heart and your all to people unless you are 100 per cent sure that they are there for you, and not to gain anything, love shouldn't cost you, truth shouldn't cost you, know you are worth so much more than you realise, I never imagined some people would leave my life, and it hurt, but there comes a point where enough is enough.

Life doesn't have to be so stressful, if your day isn't going great, talk to someone and just have a mini meltdown and get back up. I've been knocked down more times than a person should and so have a lot of people, but it doesn't really happen as much as it did before I broke through my ego, now I just think it is what it is, why fight, kick, dwell and scream for days or weeks, where will it get you? Nowhere, does the person care who abandoned you or hurt you? No, they don't, they are living their fake life not giving you a second thought, not even all the support or good you did for that person, they don't care and probably never did, so don't give your power away! Because nine times out of ten if you walk away, they will need you before you need them, and you can politely tell them where to go! Instead of saying f*** off, just say how can I help you to f*** off, be kind about everything.

I give people one chance now, if they hurt me or I see I'm being used because they can gain something from me, I don't give them a second chance, because if they really cared and loved you, they wouldn't treat you or disrespect you like they do, and that applies to everyone no matter who you are.

Like I said I'm by far perfect, nobody is, but I hold my hands up to all my mistakes, but I won't be sorry if someone feels ashamed or embarrassed about me, sorry but that's a you problem not a me problem! I don't change myself or chase after people anymore, that ship has well and truly sailed on out. I will only offer my friendship once if it's turned down that's on you not me.

At the end of the day, you haven't experienced a lot of the traumas I faced, I dealt silently alone. And one trauma I suffered, I kept quiet because I didn't want anything to happen to people I loved, because I know if I had spoken up, it could of got very dark for people, so I stayed silent, and then when I finally was able to open up, I wasn't believed by those who claimed to love me. Now I look back and I think, that's how much they thought of me, they thought that much of me that they thought I would make something like that up! It broke me, and that's when I did realise I was on my own, nobody wanted to help me through or support me, I was just a liar, and that's the biggest hurt I think I've faced, and again my feelings or what I had experienced, it didn't matter to anyone except my little family, they kept me going, I did want to give up, I had thoughts of ending it, but they kept me going, they needed me, so I swore nobody would ever make me feel that way again, because that hurt & pain crippled me. So, I don't think twice about cutting people out anymore, because they made me feel absolutely worthless, I had always been there for them, covered for them, got relationships back together, but again that doesn't matter, because it was all about them and how it made them feel. Not once did anyone give my feelings a second thought. So, it's okay to feel, it's okay to cut people out, why give your all to people who are ashamed or embarrassed by you? Don't give your power away, don't let the fear of being alone stop you from walking your path, your truth! I am not ashamed of my story, I'm not ashamed of my scars, and mostly I'm no longer ashamed of my traumas, and I will talk about my traumas if it helps someone else who desperately needs someone to actually care about them.

I thought one of my traumas could help someone, so I opened the door on it for them, but they were too wrapped up in thinking they could make a name for themselves, becoming something big, they didn't care that I had just opened up a door I sealed shut, they made me believe they understood, and I did for a minute think their compassion was real, but in reality if this was someone who had experienced a trauma like mine, the last thing you want is a whole ton of attention on you, and everyone knowing your trauma. But again, I took that as a lesson, and that's to not fall for every sob story you're given, and don't open your heart to people who don't deserve it! But the worst part about it is, people who are supposed to love me branded me a complete liar, yet believed this person and offered their support, yeah that was a real kick in the teeth for me, sent me on a big spiral, nearly drove me to pick up a drink for the first time in all those years!! That's the last time anyone will ever make me feel that way. And the person who opened my trauma, it was as I suspected from their actions, they had suffered a psychological break, I really did want to help this person to, but they also lied to me about something, which put me in a very awkward position, had I known the truth to begin with, then things wouldn't of got so bad for this person. Always be truthful, don't be ashamed to speak the truth through worry of judgement, if you've judged, they are not the people you want to be around.

I was also apparently a stirrer, according to another female this person was close to, I'm a stirrer for hearing a rumor and informing a friend of that rumor before it ripped a family apart, well I actually informed a family member I trusted, who had heard the rumors twice that day from other people, so yeah I'm a really bad person to want to protect a mother and children!

Yes, I will always be honest and truthful at all costs, that rumor did not go any further than myself after informing the family member, also an old friend of ours.

As I said I was not put on this earth to be liked, I was put here to have a human experience, took me a long time and a lot of darkness, including attempting to take my own life, yes it got that bad at one point, so you bet I bloody understand darkness and having no one who actually cares if your alive or dead.

I don't want a bunch of fake people at my funeral, crying over a version of me you remember and walked away from, yeah, no thanks!! One chance only and yes that fact is stated in my will, no fake mourners at all...

CHAPTER 10

When you stand back and look really hard at yourself, including everything you don't like about yourself, most of the things you don't like about yourself are not really your opinions, you dislike those things because of your ego, some people dented your pride, made you envious, made you feel worthless, made you want to compete, it's what the ego does, because you have been taught and shaped by society to think and be that way, when you dissolve your ego you start to love things about yourself, your ego controls your whole life, it's been used against you, to stop you from knowing and finding the power you hold inside of you, to stop you from being happy and content with who you are, to compete with others with brands, cars even homes, to stop you from seeing the true miracle that is life, to stop you knowing the real true you. So when you work on your emotions and deal with one thing at a time, you are more likely to succeed, this process can't be rushed, and you do have to face everything you don't like about yourself, but don't judge yourself, you are only human. It's time to set yourself free from what's been holding you back all these years, it's time to finally say goodbye to the past and a big welcome to the future, a brand-new start, a brand-new version of you, are you ready to make the best investment ever?? And that's in yourself, because that's another thing you do have to work on, believing in yourself, you don't need fake people just telling you what you want to hear, you want friendships where you grow together, you need that human connection, try doing this with a friend or family member, so you can help each other and inspire and encourage each other, like I've said a number of times, you can reach out to us if you are unsure about it of you need a little help!

EGO: Your ego has probably been bruised quite a few times during your life, so sometimes it makes it difficult to get back up and try again.

Ego is responsible for all our emotions; we just haven't been taught how to use it correctly.

Every time you got knocked back or a bit beaten up, you learned to do something right? So, you learned to do it a bit better, if you learn from your frustrations, then you further yourself. So, take a negative situation, put a spin on it and turn it into a lesson, what do you want to learn from it?

There is a message in each failing or mistake, if you get the message then you will learn to grow quicker, now that you are going to be tuning into the real you, you will understand things much faster, and you certainly won't hit as many bumps in the road as you do. So, stop letting your ego rule your life, break through it, we believe in you, and we believe you can achieve it!

Show us the beautiful designer you are inside, pass on these things you are learning and discovering.

Always stop and have a think; to digest all the information, you have to stop and have a think!

Love

Love is powerful, so very powerful!
Love paves the way through challenges. It illuminates the highest pathways ahead.

Love is the bridge between you and the universe, the infinite.

Love is weaved throughout every single thing, and present everywhere.

And when you return to love, you return to presence and to the recognition of the underlying harmony and wholeness of everything.

When you're in a state of love, compassion & kindness, you sync with the divine and with the highest possibilities to thrive and grow into something truly beautiful.

Write down all the things you love about yourself, really think of you and how you actually view yourself.

Hate

Hate should never really be a thing, it's a very strong and powerful word, and shouldn't be used lightly really, because with hate comes darkness, ugliness, and uncaring ways. But sadly, the word is used a lot.

Write down all the things you don't like about yourself, ask yourself why you don't like each thing, really think about it.

Pride

Another word that holds people back, they are too proud to accept help because it will dent their pride. A feeling of deep pleasure or satisfaction derived from one's own achievements, the achievements of those whom one is closely associated, or from qualities or possessions that are widely admired.

Also, consciousness of one's own dignity.

There is a pride those with egos still intact will never feel, and it's not for material things either, it's inspiring others to chase their dreams, it's taking pride in helping others grow.

List all the things that you are proud of, not material things, within yourself, your inner core, what makes you proud of you?

Guilt

Guilt is a nasty one, it makes people guilt you into doing things, just like fear, they come hand in hand, how many times have you gone out of your way to help someone because you would feel guilt if you didn't? How many people have guilt tripped you on purpose? Not really a friend if they guilt trip you on purpose, that's the reality anyway.

Or maybe you feel guilt for mistakes you made, did you learn from those mistakes? If you did then let it go, you can not go back and do it over again, so let it go, focus on what's in front of you that you can change, don't live in what's behind you, nobody was given a guide on how to live this human experience, so stop thinking of all your mistakes and focus that energy in moving forward more positively.

You can achieve it if you do the work. Many have already gone through this process, and we know it does work.

Grief

This is a very difficult one, and as already spoken about in previous chapters, you don't have to let go of the person you loved or cared about, but you do have to let all the pain & hurt in, you can try to distract yourself, but as I've learnt recently, distracting yourself only prolongs the inevitable, and when you do let it in, it hit's harder, and you fall back further, so let it all in, and you will slowly learn to swim again. And they are waiting for us. But people can really become lost in grief, but ask yourself, would that person you loved want you to stop living? Absolutely not, they would want you to honor them by living your life, life will never be the same, there will always be a hole where that person used to be, but you can be happy, you are allowed to be happy again. There is no crime in grieving for that person while still living life.

Jealousy/ Envy

This one has always had me stumped, why the jealousy of others or the envy?? Both are just horrible ugly words! When you are jealous of a best friend, it's not really a best friend is it? Best friends don't do jealousy, they inspire and support you, they are loyal, loving and honest, you care for each other for the people you are, not what you can get out of it or gain from it. It's not healthy at all to be jealous of another's life or possessions, it's just things, and things that don't really matter, I can say I've never been jealous of anyone's life, I wouldn't want fame because that's me, I'm not a lime light person, everything I do is done with love or comes from a place of love, as a team we do not do jealousy, we don't think any of us are better than any other team member, we are all equal, and that's what connects us.

Embarrassment/ shame.

These are painful emotions of humiliation or distress caused by the consciousness of wrong or foolish behavior, regrettable or unfortunate situations or actions.

If people try to make you feel shame for your actions or embarrassed about something you choose to wear that they don't think suit's you, but you feel confident and happy wearing it, you don't need friends like that. You want people who see past the material things, people who see you, your beautiful heart, your selflessness, they cheer you on, encourage you to just be you, nothing more nothing less, friendship shouldn't cost, it should come with love, loyalty and respect, things that do not cost you anything.

Write down everything you feel embarrassed about or things you are ashamed of, work through each one, asking why did it make you feel that way? Why did it affect you that way? Why did you act that way? What did it change, you feeling that way? You have to break everything down and find the route cause, only then will you break the pattern of where you are going wrong.

Trust / loyalty

These are huge emotions when broken, damaging emotions! I've learnt through working hard on myself that trust is an honor not to be abused, and that if you expect loyalty, real loyalty, you have to be TRUTHFUL always. Since about 2 years ago, everything people confided in me has stayed with me, not that I told peoples secrets I will admit before I may of spoke to my eldest daughter about things, but that changed as I grew, so everyone who has confided in me in the last 2 year's, it's stayed with me and only me, I won't break anyone's trust because my trust was blown to pieces by people who claimed to love me, and it was awful, and then I hear they are telling people things I confided in them, and it really hurt, these are people I had shown support, love and respect to, yet they never cared, and that was a big wake up call for me.

So, you have to look at yourself again, and ask, why don't you trust? Why would you be disloyal? What did you gain from not being loyal? What did you gain from breaking someone's trust? Every bad part of you, you have to face.

Lies / Betrayal

Well, I thought I knew betrayal but sadly I was wrong, lies and betrayal are the worst! And I don't understand why people make stuff up, like I said I'm an open book, a friendship of mine disappeared, and boy was I shocked to hear this friend had been spreading a rumor around that I had slept with her dad, I was absolutely gob smacked! I'm some things or used to be some things but that was absolute bulls**t, and it really hurt and made me physically sick.

I had looked after this friends children for a few years for free, while they were working, earning money, this same friend told someone who was growing weed, that I had called the police on them, they threatened my daughter, and put us through hell, we happened to be in a pub at the same time, so I asked this friend, go and ask him who this friend of mine was who had informed them it was me who grassed them up, but she wouldn't and the panic on their face said everything, so that was all I needed to know, that feeling in the pit of my stomach was correct, it was devastating really.

And another friend who I took under my wing, cared for, even loved, nearly ruined a friends relationship by spreading false lies, they nearly split over these lies and I was devastated, yes the friend came to see me and told me, I was quite happy to talk to his girlfriend to tell her it was not true, I was in a relationship with my other half, but he said it was best left, and thankfully it didn't ruin his relationship, all I ever wanted was to see him happy, in love with his soul mate, we had history, nobody knew us, we were both broken people, and we weren't meant for each other, we were both happy that we both found our soul mates in the end, I loved seeing him happy with his family, we remained friends, real nasty person aren't I?? So, if you lie or gossip about people, ask yourself why? Does it make you happy? Does it make you feel more superior to the person you are slating?

So, I do have boundaries I don't cross! Do you ever stop to think that your lies and your spreading of false information could lead to someone wanting to end their life? Because I wanted to end mine over these false accusations, I didn't want to be here anymore I wouldn't wish for anyone to end their life if I liked them or not, I would stop someone I didn't like from doing it and probably end up liking the person they become, because I would do everything to help them get back on their feet.

So strip yourself back, face the things you did wrong and focus on being a more supportive positive person, to those you claim to care about, this life is to busy is rubbish, if you can write a lengthy Facebook status, you can drop your friend a how are you, but no your fake status is more important, because in fact you are not a supportive friend at all, you just want others to think you are? How is that a healthy happy life?

Compassion / Honesty

These two emotions come hand in hand, especially for Empaths, our compassion is something else. Compassion means you are very sympathetic of other's, their emotional well-being matters to you, the misfortune they suffer, you just want to help, but you have to be honest, and not be afraid to raise your voice if someone is treating you wrong, this also brings trust back in, it's like I always say, I would rather stand alone and be truthful, than be fake and pretend you matter, friendships & relationships shouldn't ever be one sided.

So, when looking at yourself here, you have to ask yourself, why do I never speak my truth? Why can't I just be honest and say how I feel? Why do you carry so much compassion for people who don't give the same back? Why am I not compassionate and honest? It's the awkward questions you have to ask to be able to see your worth.

Wisdom is always available to you, but only if you are open to it. You don't need to strive for peace or advice because it's there inside of you. Treat yourself with more compassion and honesty, trust in yourself.

Trust yourself to find the best possible life out there.

Fear / scared

These two are the biggest and weakest emotions we have, and they have been used against us our whole lives sadly, people fear dying, people fear change, people fear how society looks at them, so you have to face your fear here, write everything down you are fearful of or scared of.

Why am I afraid to comment on someone's status when I agree with it 100%? I bet it's because it's someone like me and you're worried how it will look to others? Why are you so fearful of what others think of you? Why are you worried about what you look like to others? Why are you scared to tell someone when you don't agree with them? Why are you scared of ghosts? That's a common one, there is nothing to fear, it's the way so called true stories are portrayed, it's how you have been taught, your belief system is completely programmed wrong, you will find most honest successful people, they don't fear anything, they are very humble in what they do, like Keanu Reeves, he has money, yet he prefers to look like someone homeless, he isn't afraid of what he looks like, Mel Gibson, he wasn't afraid to speak his truth even though they ruined his reputation and branded him as crazy, but he made his film, he was determined to share his truth and if you haven't watched it, the sound of freedom is the name, about Hollywood and it's not so nice side. The very idols and influencers you look up to, doing and committing awful crimes and the worst part, getting away with it.

They will always use your fear to control you, usually using death, the number one fear, break through it, if it's going to happen you can't stop it, so live everyday like your last, make sure the people you love, know how much you love them, reach out to that person who just feels like you hate them, because someone I looked up to my whole life, couldn't even look at me, and that hurt really bad, but they won't ever make me feel that way ever again!

I can still love & care for people and cut them off, I just don't let them hold any power over my emotions anymore, because they are not worth my tears, maybe one day they may apologize for making me feel that way, and maybe not, I'm okay either way.

I don't fear not having these people in my life anymore, not like I used to, and they have no idea of the battles I've fought these past couple year's, they knew a version of me that no longer exists, she is in the past where she belongs, with all the mistakes she made, this version hasn't made any mistakes so far, and I'm keeping it that way!

The thing with FEAR is it holds you in it's claws, but truthfully it's you who traps yourself! Don't worry about failing or making mistakes, because they are your lessons, treat them that way. When you look back on your life, especially the hardest parts, you understand there was a lesson to be learnt from that, when you have more awareness and control over your emotions, that's when you break free.

Don't be afraid to make mistakes because you are now on a

path of great growth & ascension and you have to trust in that fact. Trust in yourself.

You strip your fears back and what scares you most, and you become quite a force. But most importantly, you become fearless, and life gets exciting when you get through the whole ego issue!

The best thing I did was break through fear, I'm an open book and will admit to my mistakes, I have nothing to hide! Yes I've used real life experiences, they are mine, if the friends responsible for causing those problems for me read this, when all I ever did was support and care about them, I really hope you have changed, and I don't want no apology or to humiliate you, not at all, your actions caused me and my family issues, hurt and pain, my child was threatened over your lies, and I never ever made up false accusations about you. The worse thing is you did these things while we were still friends...The truth always comes out, but I still wish you well in life, and maybe if you hadn't been dishonest, karma wouldn't keep paying you a visit.

Chapter 11

It is up to you to put all this information we are revealing to practice. Once you do, and you start to realize for yourself, all the benefit's it does come with, and you start to feel your vibration rise, you will keep going and rising, because you will know and have your own proof, that what we have all achieved, it does actually work and change your whole life. Grow and watch how incredible you become.

You have to go through every uncomfortable moment in your life, strip all the emotions back and find the route cause, and I will tell you now, most people's fears are from some childhood trauma, we all have an inner child that always needed love, support, and something happened whether you remember it or not, but something changed you, so you are always trying to protect that inner child, when really all you need to do is break through your ego, and become the support that, that younger you needed and go rescue you!

Bring the real you back! It's time, if you are tired of your own crap, you can turn your whole life around, it's all layer out for you, the stages the questions to ask yourself, I may have missed questions, I'm basing the questions off myself and the team.

You may have some deep routed trauma like myself, but you can finally beat it and start living, live, laugh and love, be happy, stop letting the rich rob you blind, and start thinking of yourself, because if you are one of these people who literally give your child everything they want, then they will never appreciate life properly, because you are distracting their minds with technology instead of showing them the beauty of life itself, change has to start from within.

Living a life where you take the kids to school, pop to a friends to have a good gossip about someone else's misfortune or something they posted, go home, do housework, tea and then bed and rinse and repeat, or if you go to work, but still pop to a friend's just to talk about other people, ask yourself, do you actually have anything in common apart from talking about others?? As I've said, some people who spout they support mental health are absolute hypocrites if your bashing down other people, I know all too well the toll mental health takes on a person, but I took the time to learn and understand, and the root cause of my mental health was the way people made me feel, and that's awful, I would be horrified if I found out I had caused someone so much hurt that they tried to end their own life.

Where has people's common decency gone? Where are people's morals? It used to be help thy neighbor, now it's neighbors at war, what are you not seeing?? you have to take a long hard look in the mirror and fix the reflection, only when we changed what they have made us become, can we all bring about change for our future generations.

Nobody is coming along on a white horse to fix the world, we have to fix what we all broke, because that is the truth, we all broke the world by falling for what we thought was best for us, for being sold one lie after another, and we bought every single lie, well most did, fortunately some were already awake to try to slow down all the plans that they have for us.

It's time to pull your heads out the technology and really look around at what the world has become, there are less jobs in supermarkets because technology is slowly taking over, people don't even need to walk to the shop anymore, it can be delivered to your door at a small cost of course, I have to try to do something to stop us being led into a dark & out right evil world.

I have to try to get you to see the illusion you have been sold, a 3d world, which it isn't once you dissolve your ego, it's a whole new beautiful world, and man is ruining it.

And we are doing nothing to stop it, once cash is gone, there won't be any stashing for a rainy day, what if your account gets hacked and you can't buy anything? Or you go over your allowance of what you are allowed to spend? Do you not see how dangerous and the impact it could have on people, sadly suicide rates will climb even higher, so you will have blood on your hands.

I really feel for all the parents who lost children from the new medical treatment for covid, so many parents left with huge guilt, well if you are one of those parents, please don't blame yourselves, it wasn't your fault at all, we were heavily manipulated and our fear was used against us, I'm still baffled as to why there are no crimes against humanity charges happening to these people in power, even our own police force protect these awful human's, when really the police should be the first to take a stand, after all they all swore an oath, just like medical professionals, their incentives to push this new treatment, was
£15 a pop! Imagine the money our go surgeries made... Stop letting fear & money be your rulers, it's the only way to truly find freedom I can't take credit for this next bit, but I wanted to include it, because I want you to think long and hard about what it's saying...

Did you know....

The wizard of Oz... This is very interesting.

The straw man represents that fictional ALL CAPS legal fiction - The PERSON. He wanted a brain and got a certificate - The birth certificate.

The Tin man - The TIN (Taxpayer identification number) He was a robotic avatar, who worked tirelessly until his whole body literally froze up & stopped functioning. The heartless & emotionless robot creature who worked himself to death because he had no heart or soul.

The Cowardly lion was a bully but was actually a true coward when someone stood up to him, like most bullies. He lacked true courage and in the end, the wizard gave him an official recognition Award - Authority & Status.

The wizard of Oz used magic, smoke, flames, and holograms, but all were tricks and illusions to push fear & compliance to make people do what he commanded. The Truth is the wizard has NO real power & only uses illusions to create false power and authority.

The Wicked witch pushed fear through intimidation. She was after Toto and controlled the flying monkey police, the policy enforcers, the mischievous demons, which also represent the BAR Association who attack and control all the little people for the great crown wizard, the crooked bankers of Oz, obsessed with Gold.

In the field of poppies, they were not REAL humans, so drugs had no effect on them, but Dorothy got drugged.

The wizard of Oz was written at the time when Rockefeller & The big pharma companies began to take over medicine & education.

The Crown was actually the largest drug dealer & after their take-over of drug distribution in China, they began to expand all around the world.

Toto was what the wicked witch was really after. TOTO in Latin means "in total" Toto exposed the wizard of Oz and had no fear, despite being very small compared to the Great Wizard, so no one noticed him.

Toto pulled back the curtain on the wizard of Oz, and his magical scams.

'Curtain' also means the End of an act or scene! He pulled the curtain back and started barking until others paid attention, hypothetically giving everyone the red pill.

The curtain hid the corporate legal fiction & it's false courts. So, no matter how small your bark is, it can be heard.
Stop letting fear control you, we give fear way too much power over us, and it's time for us to work out exactly who we really are, because really none of us do know who we are, not until you actually work on yourself, and I will say one thing, I used to hate being alone when kids were at school and my partner at work, but I would give anything to have those days back, because I get the chance to grow and learn more.

When I grow the whole team grows, it's pretty freaky how connected we are, but we will help people if they don't quite understand something, we will be there if you slip, you're rewiring your brain to how it should be when you entered this world, so it is a scary move, but you have 10 of us who have achieved this plus more people I have helped one to one, so we know this process does work, but only if you want it to, and you want to experience truly living fear free and humble.

Chapter 12

Its not a real book without an Ali rant...Although some may think I've had a few rants in this book, they are not, it's me calmly speaking.

So, I have this habit of having a little rant about the world when I'm live, so my supporters would be gutted if the book didn't have an Ali rant in it lol.

When you go down this route of becoming complete, it does have a lot of ups & downs at the beginning, but the harder you work on yourself, the better version you will become, and if you have children especially, working on yourself will also benefit them, because as your vibration starts to climb, it's strange but your whole household rises to, it's pretty incredible, and your teaching your children a better way, and most importantly, to never be ashamed of who they are or who they want to be. It's the best gift you can give them, you become more understanding, and they become way more relaxed, and they open up about things instead of keeping it inside.

Our children are the future, and their children will be the next, so we should be doing everything within our power to make it up to them for us falling for the technology trap, we did it first!

We don't have to sacrifice our lives like our ancestors did, we just have to wake up and start to stand up for the world we deserve, not live a life that's dictated to us by those in control, because it shouldn't be one rule for them and another for us, even our police don't protect the public anymore, they protect those in power and their agenda, I don't know how anyone can go against an oath for corrupt people, I don't know how anyone can accept money and other things to inflict pain on other's, I would be telling them to stick their job, no amount of money would make me want to harm another person, if it's someone evil I will do it for free lol.

Where are the men these days, especially in the police force and other services?? Because back in the good days, a man would do anything and everything to protect their wife and children, they would give their own lives for them, but men are just sitting back, not all men, there are some fighting, but I see more women than men fighting, technology has made man weak, yes I will use weak here, where's your balls to fight for a better future? You're going along with all this absolute nonsense, what could happen if all the men took a stand against the corruption going on in front of your eyes, and you're working your ass off to pay for this corruption, it's absolutely mind boggling really, if you are a man reading this come on!!!! I intend on fighting for a better future until my time comes, or someone knocks me off, I'm not afraid of dying or death, it's just a process, you get used to it, how can you look your children in the eyes later on when your whole life is dictated to you, when they talk of the old world, how can you look at them and say you did NOTHING to fight for their futures, just how??, I have more fight in me than most men, because I'm not controlled and consumed by FEAR.

What is it you're actually frightened of? Giving your life for your child's, shouldn't that be at the top of your list? Because I can look my children in the eyes and say I did my best, I gave my all to fight for a better world, I haven't stopped fighting since 2020 and I don't intend to, I will go to my grave fighting, if you're not going to fight for your children, then why did you have them? It makes absolutely no sense to me at all.

Being born in the 1970's I had the best childhood and teenage years, no internet, no sky tv, no mobile phones, we had to go to a friend's house to see if they were coming out, which is exercise as well, we knew when the street lights came on we had to go in, we didn't have any fear back then, we made our own fun, we had that human interaction, we learnt from our elders, we had it so good. Most of the children these days are learning from influencers on social media, gangs, 14-year-olds are carrying knifes for gods' sake, what do you not see?? These influencers shouldn't even be allowed on social media, why do you think they do allow it? Surely I don't have to spell it out!

So stop moaning on social media and do something about it, if your child is a known trouble maker, work on yourself so you can save them from themselves, we have a generation of very confused children, and nobody is standing up for them, you're going along with three ridiculous names and explanations, don't you see where this is heading, something will be known as normal before long and it makes me sick to my stomach just hearing the name or about it, I'm in no way against anyone, any race or colour, I love humanity, but really?

I've never witnessed such a generation of very messed up confused children and that is heartbreaking, how can you do nothing! And this also does apply to any parent who is walking around wearing a blindfold because your likes on your latest social media post are more important, or how many followers you have, why does it matter about likes and follows? I don't understand that either, not one bit, if I put a post up, I'm not checking every 10 minutes on how it's doing, it will do however it will.

I did it for me mainly so I can look back in a few years and see how much more I've grown and for our paranormal pages, it's just highlights from a live that one of our supporters might have missed really! I don't rush to chuck something up either, I do it when I have time, it's not on my list of priorities, like now writing this, we captured something mind blowing, but I'm writing this, that clip can wait, I haven't put a clip up for a few days actually, I'm just loving learning and helping people reach their full potential, loving life, it is what it is at the end of the day, and what will be will be, we can't look back, but we can learn a better way and change the future, because we do owe our children that much. And don't get me wrong, my children are my world, but if I knew we would be living in a world like this, I wouldn't of had children, we need to do better and that includes anyone who doesn't have them, we had the best childhoods, they deserve that to, it's to late for some, but the young ones now they deserve our fight, and if you disagree with that, then you really don't have a heart or any humanity so you can't be helped because your to selfish and probably would never break through your ego!

And I won't apologize for that last statement. I think that's what I loved the most about Michael Jackson and Princess Diana, their compassion for humanity always stood out to me, there was something unique about them that I did admire, and Michael Jackson got put through the ringer, when all he wanted to do was protect children, because he knew what went on, and I think Diana did too. I haven't seen any compassion like it in anyone else for children especially in a long time.

But for humanity, Mel Gibson and Keanu Reeves are my top ones, such selfless acts of kindness they give, and I know they see the world pretty much the same way we do. Although recently I did hear something a little disturbing, I'm yet to research that for myself, as I do with everything.

The children are the future, they are not little soldiers, the education system is getting ridiculous, we all turned out okay without this ridiculous levels of homework they get that none of us understand, being sent to exclusion rooms for dropping pencils, it's insane, you're allowing your child to be abused in schools now mentally!

It's like life, if a friend walked up to you and said there is someone who tells me when I can go out, and when I do I have to be covered up, they monitor my bank account, they watch my every move, and if I don't do as they say I don't get any money or food, I have to do everything they say, I have to work 3 jobs and they take most of my money off me, and I'm left with hardly anything!

You would advise them it's an abusive relationship right? You would tell them they need to get away and get out of it right?

Now apply that to what those in power are doing to us, don't you see it? But because they are in power it's allowed right? It's acceptable for them to abuse us...I really don't understand at all.

It's literally like standing in a dessert waiting for rain, but then they can make it rain now and destroy crops, so can't really use that. Another so-called conspiracy theory about them controlling the weather that's come out as true! Start standing up it's quite easy really!

Because if you're not standing up, if you are just going to go along with whatever they tell you to, why are you here? Are you going to spend your human experience being told what to do because you are scared? And that's not meant in a horrible way, I'm just trying to get you to see that you do have a purpose here, and there is a reason you are here right now!

So knowledge up and start making a difference, because if we all tried to make a difference together, at least we would get somewhere, even if we failed, at least we tried, and you can look your child in the eyes and say, "We all did try our best, and we fought hard" doesn't that sound better than "I didn't fight for you at all" ?? So, I will leave it there for you to seriously think about it, I know your Ego has probably been dented reading that, but it's the truth, and sometimes you have to hurt for people to wake up and heal, but as one not divided!!

How did I come to discover all the corruption, it's pretty easy, you follow the money, it always leads back to the same people, change can only happen for the better if you are willing and determined to stamp out your Ego, life is so much nicer & easier without one, you don't get offended like you used to, you don't overthink, you don't fear things that haven't even happened.

I see people do statutes about struggling but when I offer my help it's always "I'm okay I will sort it out" why are you attention seeking? Because that's what it is if you're not willing to do anything to change it? Does people commenting oh I'm sorry etc., how does that change how you feel if that is in fact how you are feeling, because I know when I was offered help I took all the help I could get, and I never thought I would ever feel this happy in life, after trying to be accepted for half my life, I finally feel I do belong here, I don't have dark days anymore, I don't need to be surrounded by people who don't really care, I don't need my FB posts to be liked, I really don't care, because I post for ME, not for others, I was asked to do some songs for someone I helped, someone who supported me from the moment I stepped onto TikTok, so I decided to do a couple videos and stick the songs on my fb, but I did it for me and my girls, so when I'm no longer here, they will always have my voice, those memories of me, knowing I gave my all to everything I did, but most people with their ego firmly intact will probably think "she thinks she's amazing" or "god she loves herself" or some stupid ridiculous ego comment, because you don't ever look at the bigger picture or the feelings or the example, I want my grandson to know his Nan was fearless, I gave everything a go, I'm certainly no Taylor swift, don't want to be anything like her thanks, but I did those songs for someone I cared about, he had a list, I didn't get to finish that list before he passed, but a promise is a promise and I will finish that list, because now I know those songs were carefully picked to also make me learn something, it's a gift from someone who was robbed of his life, for an experiment!! His words not mine! Someone who also wished they had known me in 2020, we met halfway through 2021 when we started live streaming, I didn't live stream for the first year on TikTok, but he taught me a thing or two as well.

In order for the world to be a better place, everyone needs to pull their heads out of the technology trap and focus time on changing yourself, technology could have been great if used correctly, but everyone fell for the trap, and in doing so they made you lazy, disrespectful, no regard for humanity, greedy and competitive!

You can't say any different, because you are living life like it's a competition, look at me I drive a Merc! I got all the latest iPhone technology, do you know how sad you sound, complain about money but spend over £20,000 on a bloody car!! Really?? You've been heavily manipulated and controlled, whether you except that fact or not, it is the truth. Will people show you more respect because you drive that shiny expensive car?? Absolutely not, but it's got heated seats and sat nav, used to manage okay in an old banger and trusty roadmap!! You're still not seeing how lazy they have made you?? Everything at the touch of a button and you can speed up the damage to your brain with those wireless air pods, you should see the readings on an EEG meter, it's quite scary, and you allow that on your children, and you wonder why cancer has risen so drastically since technology, if they wanted to cure cancer they would, but in you donating for how many years now? Or in all the years cancer research has been going, you would think they would have a cure by now surely?? Oh, they know how to cure it, but there will be too much MONEY lost in chemo and radiation therapy plus all the other crap, so it won't ever be cured, yet they can cure dieses that haven't even been discovered yet!! How amazing is that!

Enough is enough and it is time to unhook yourself from the matrix, those films certainly explain life, are you ready to change? For your children and future generations? Or do you not want them to experience the life we had, I'm 50 next year, and I don't like the world we are heading into because people are too lazy to fight back.

I haven't been wrong yet! And that's not a bragging statement, remember I do not hold an ego!

I do not think I'm better than anyone else, I'm also not ashamed that I live in a Council house, because that's always been judged upon or people feel embarrassed to admit they live in a council house, why? You don't take your house with you when you die so what does it matter?? It's your own pride being dented through your ego, that's what that is. At least you have a home, be grateful for what you do have, there are way less fortunate people around than you living in a council house, honestly the mind control is astounding!

And please remember, I have no ego so I'm not having a go at anyone or a pop, everything I'm saying comes from a place of love & concern for humanity! I'm just trying to get you to see how you have been manipulated and tricked!

Yes change has to happen to make progress, but not in the evil way the powers in charge want, they don't stand a chance if everyone united, look at things they have done in other countries, they are fighting, yet the UK people do nothing, well not all of us, but there needs to be more to bring about good changes, not evil twisted changes.

I am no racist, and I have nothing against how people want to dress or anything like that, but tax payers money was being spent on the police escorting cross dressers to libraries to read to toddler's, you have no idea of that persons background, so I'm not being judgy, but that was wrong, children need help because they are more confused than ever on what they are or who they should be, it's so wrong! Why are parents not standing up for their children's mental health, you see teenagers dressed up acting like cats and people accept it as normal, it's not normal at all... These things are thought up by sick minds then influencers are PAID well to push it out! Wake the hell up before it gets worse.

Suicide rates and mental health are at an all-time high since covid, and nobody seems to care??

It is like living a real-life circus, they are making a mockery out of everyone, and you are allowing it to happen, which makes it worse!

That's my rant over, but I hope it's made you have a proper think, because if this was Tom Cruise or someone else telling you this, you would listen and that's where the real problem lies, between your idols and influencers, it's that simple! And it's that sad.

Think what you will of me, I am well past caring, like I said, this isn't for everyone and only the strong will see it and achieve breaking through their ego.

Always be humble not a bragger, because bragging isn't a good look on anyone, no matter who you are Teach your children respect, give them your time, not a new iPhone or laptop, we have to get out of this trap, and making a future where our children will be happy and loved, everything needs to change, the Justice system literally everything, I'm sorry but murders and rapists should get the death penalty, not a second chance at life, when most that come out supposedly changed and reformed, they end up doing it again, when they shouldn't be allowed a second chance at all, maybe the world would be safer if the death penalty was given to more serious offenders!

Honestly, I had a friend sent to prison for something stupid, yet two men who assaulted a woman, well they got a fine and community service, how is that right? So, once they have done their community service, they are free to attack someone else, that's a really fantastic justice system right there. All judges who have and do take back handers to turn the other way, all high-ranking police officers who have been informed more than enough about crimes against humanity being committed, and they are doing nothing about it! So, if you have status, power and money, you can commit murder and not even get a slap on the wrist, brilliant world we live in.

We need people with love, compassion and truth running the country not people who just see power and money! They all invested in these new treatments, all got wealthy from people dying, how is that right?? Got to see their loved ones too, when most didn't get to say goodbye to theirs, or had to through a screen, all while those in power were having parties, they had all the data, and they broke all the rules they gave us! And still no outrage, still no one fighting for what's right, fighting for justice for the people who didn't get to pass surrounded by their loved ones! They stole those last moments from you!

Where is your fight?? And if you are still rolling up your sleeve you are part of the real reason we are walking into a nightmare!

I say it as it is, like I said, I'm not here to be popular or famous, that lifestyle makes me physically sick! Caroline Flack got pushed over the edge by the media, well where is the media exposing all the corruption going on?? They won't because they too are owned and controlled.

Only an honest person will want the best for you, will care about you, and will love you, so don't settle for anything less than you truly deserve.

Break through your ego and start living and loving in a whole new way, I wouldn't go back to my old version for millions of pounds, I am the best version I've ever been, and all I want is for people to experience the same freedom we feel, this change will cost you your comfort zone, friendships even, but believe me, it will be worth it in the end. When you truly find you, that's when life really begins for you.

Build a future to be proud of and leave a legacy for your children.

Chapter 13

There is a real beautiful potential now to deeply activate the higher levels of yourself, your light.

Step into embodying the fullness of your unique, authentic self, as a divine spiritual being in physical form.

Activations are usually on the other side of release.

So, if you are experiencing lower levels of emotion, past painful experiences with family or friends, or problems with self-worth.

Just breathe, love yourself through the process, and know that letting go and releasing the past allows you to fiercely step into the new you.

Embrace who you were always supposed to be, embrace the reason you are in this world at this moment in time, in history.

It's been a right whirlwind month for us, yet amidst all the challenging and unsettled energy, we are feeling a pull more than ever to level up, raise our vibration and step in to more of who we are, who we truly are.

Enjoy your awareness to expand and the qualities of the divine to anchor within your field through your chakra energy centers, for your benefit and in the highest interest of all.

There are big energies coming, big changes unfolding, it's all happening for us.

But the journey is not always easy, and I'm ever grateful for the support and guidance that right on divine timing continues to appear.

This is a very powerful time for observing the vibrant life force energy building and growing in the earth, and then claiming the power of this time by planting seeds, and consciously manifesting positive changes in life.

This really is a time to break free from old, outdated patterns, patterns that clearly don't work. You need to look from different perspectives of who you thought you were,

This is a powerful time for clearing distorted, heavy, and outdated energies and thought patterns and emotional pathways that just no longer serve you.

Clearing and healing suffering from this lifetime, from collective consciousness, and across the lines of time. Remember the Truth.

You are light, you are love, you are a divine being with the ability to observe, and bring whatever arises in your energy field into the light of love where it can be transmuted and alchemized into something new and exciting.

Calling forward the qualities and energy that will serve.
Calling forward greater love, peace, and truth.
A note from a Guardian angel (oracle cards)

New doors are opening for you to step into peace and harmony with your highest divine path.

One step and one moment at a time, you have the opportunity to choose to be in alignment with the path of joy, and higher frequency now available to you.

Choose the path of love over fear. Be the pilar of light you came here to be. Allow the grace of the divine, the love frequency woven throughout the infinite to reach you.

This is such a good time to consciously drop into love and presence, amidst the continued waves of transformation and new beginnings.

There are changes happening within humanity, but simultaneously, this time of year is potent as the forces of life within the earth powerfully stir.

You need to gently release things that no longer serve you, raise your vibration and send out an astonishing wave of love, light, peace, and well-being through your reality and to benefit all.

How you respond to change and challenge now has the opportunity to be updated if you allow it.

We're human beings, which means there are always going to be faced with challenges & changes, there is no way around this.

And we've all learned ways of dealing with change and challenges, for better or worse,

So now when you're presented with some change or challenge in reality you may get triggered to automatically respond to it in an old "low vibe" or outdated way.

(With doubt, fear, judgement, unhealthy habit's, or stress related patterns that are somehow related to past trauma, programs, or wounding) But with presence and awareness, you have the choice!

Do you repeat the old pattern on autopilot, giving in to fear and uncertainty?

Or do you notice old patterning beginning to play out, observe it, and pause the spiral of mind and fear, so you can consciously release underlying emotional wounding and choose to respond in a new and empowering way.

Personally, I would highly recommend the second option, but of course each person is different, this is not often easy at all, so when you do fall or slip up, shift!

Breathe, step back and observe your situation from a higher state of consciousness.

You are a human being, but you are also full of light. Choose to break free from the past patterns that weigh you down and hold you back, they keep you stuck in old ways.

Always respond in an empowering way, from a different perspective, you deserve the best of what life has to offer.

And exactly how your life is right now, you do have a lot to be extremely grateful for so lean into these things.

When you stay in alignment with love and happiness, you truly do support the highest possibilities for life. So, in future when a challenge or situation arises, pay attention to how you respond, is it love, or fear based?

How can you respond to this in a new way?

How can you respond in a way that resonates with love?

Call in the help of your angels, we all have them, just waiting for us to connect so they can guide us, ask the angels to release old energies and remember that you can shift in any moment.

Now is the time to bring your spiritual power into the physical, one choice at a time.

As you do, your vibration rises, and you experience more love, joy, and peace, honestly they feel so new and exciting!

This is a time of huge change, challenge, and transformation on Earth.

Which you as a soul actually chose to be here for by the way. (our research tells us this)

Cultivate that love and compassion within to help guide you through.

And whether effortlessly riding the waves of light, or feeling challenged and thrown around in emotional storms, remember that you are not alone! We're all in this together and one moment at a time we can make a huge difference by consciously holding the love, light, and peace around the planet.

Release the old and let the new levels of love in!

And it's okay to have doubt, but trust in yourself, trust how this makes you feel, does this make you feel excited? To discover who you truly are, does it ignite something deep within you? Maybe this feeling is new...But if I have learnt one thing on this journey of mystery, magic, exciting adventures, it's to always listen to those instincts, don't ever ignore those!

And hopefully you will have experienced these feelings in your life to know what to watch out for, if you get an odd or weird vibe, it's not for you.

Not everyone will achieve dissolving their ego, a lot of people won't see where we are coming from, they will instantly be hurt, because a lot can't except constructive criticism, not even when it can change your whole entire life for the better, so if you have made it this far, then things are resonating with you, and maybe you are ready to truly break the illusion, break the fear and finally be ego free, like I've said over & over, it really is a whole new level of living which I never thought was possible, not ever! So, if I can do this and my team can do this, then so can you, or if you don't do anything, we can say we tried, we tried to make a difference in the world, we tried to show people how to truly live!

It's normal to have a little fear when working on yourself, but honestly, it's not really difficult, it's a lot of writing and thinking for yourself.

They don't want us to remember who we truly are, they don't want us to discover the wisdom and power that has been buried deep within us by years of conditioning and programming.

They don't want us to wake up, but we must!

So much is happening right now...You could be feeling some kind of pressure.

Stop what you are doing when you feel yourself becoming despondent, bring awareness to it then, take a deep breath in, pause, imagine that all your thoughts are melting into your heart, exhale, be still...Then, choose wisely.

What if you could significantly reduce painful life lessons, growing equally as well, through joyful life lessons instead? It is possible and it is within everyone's reach.

With this year's summer solstice came a great ascension shift, so it's a great time to put our methods into practice, you will move forward with monumental life changes. And because of this you'll encounter resistance, in the form of you pushing back at your progress and also in the form of others pushing against you.

If you can relate to this then you know - You'll never encounter resistance if you never start something new. Resistance is the fuel that helps you fly.

Just imagine a time on earth where people everywhere honoured, respected, upheld and called upon the feminine aspect of nature. The Goddess was a key component of sacred, divine connection in nearly every ancient culture on earth. We used to openly speak with her in our temples and homes, ask her for assistance and align with the wisdom, strength and all-knowing leadership of the cosmic feminine.

This new energy this year, especially for Empaths, has certainly been a rollercoaster ride of strong energies, causing us to become more eternal and physically sensitive to fluctuations in subtle energy. Star alignments are very intensive.

In short words, you could feel emotional for no clear reason, you could be feeling the pain of the world. You could be reminiscing about the past and assessing the deeper meaning of your life.

I absolutely love this quote; Every moment is an opportunity to let the flow take you to the best possible outcome.

So, you can either raise the energy levels right now, or you can decide to embrace new and innovative approaches to your life.
That's the way of the soul. It's your personality that sticks to the past and the known. Soul loves the new!

Hence, why your painful lessons can keep repeating. You can consciously change them, by employing a fresh approach each day. Who's for less painful lessons, it all begins now....

Trust what you are hearing is wisdom straight for you. Your path will look completely different from someone else's, remember we are all different and unique in our own ways, and that's okay because they have their way, and you have yours. You have a difference in flavour.

The creator wanted each of us to follow our specific path for love, joy, and abundance.

In helping each other, you also find great peace and joy for helping another on their path, can indeed be a path all on it's own, the greatest thing you can do, is help guide another, if they themselves are lost to guidance. Open up your heart to receive the freedom you long for.

You long to do a deeply passionate thing, that's because it's installed in you to be a joyful being. You are called to be higher than you are now, and you have to raise your joy levels.

In joy you receive, be fresh, be free, and stop holding yourself captive to your fears.

The greatest weapon that is formed against you is simply one word: FEAR. It tries to hold you in it's claws, but really, it's you who traps yourself.

Don't worry about failing or making mistakes because they are your lessons. Treat them as such. Don't be afraid to make them because you are still on the path of abundance. Trust the fact. Wisdom is always available to you if you are open to it.

You really don't have to strive for peace or advice, most of the time, the answers are inside us, we just need to step back at look at it from different perspectives.

Ride past the negativity in your life. Cast out anything that has made you feel discouraged in the past. You must wipe the slate clean completely in your mind (remember we are correcting your belief system to how it should be; not what society has created) as if you've never tried before. Your craft is very unique, because you are unique to this earth.

Your time here is so very precious, (most have forgotten that sadly) keep going, keep moving forward always. When you hesitate, that's when you grow weary, it's in the doing that you will be filled with wisdom. If you are stuck in what you love to do, simply take a deep breath, and ask your angels for the directions to take. (We all have angels, guides watching out for us, they will help when asked, but you have to break through the ego to fully open up to seeing signs.)

Start with somewhere you can build, build people who truly love you, love to uplift you on this journey of self-discovery. Believe that it is possible that others will support you in love. We are here to uplift you as well, all our inboxes are always open, we are happy to help.

Start where you're at, at this moment, look hard and think about everything you have read, I know it's scary when you discover what's been done to us, but please don't dwell on it, we have the opportunity to change your future, for the better, and you won't be alone, because we will set something up on our Facebook page as a support kind of place, you can stick questions on and we will answer as best we can and always honestly to.

You are beautiful, I encourage you to see yourself as such. I know it feels difficult to rise above the fears that eat at you. People can be very cruel and mean. Don't let their fear control you in your beautiful creative abilities. Look at yourself with life flowing ideas.

There are ideas just waiting for you to receive. It's like a tree growing every fruit you need in order to move forward. Pluck the fruit from the tree and receive it. Don't be afraid anymore.

I know all too well things can hurt, and hurt really bad, but please look beyond your pain and tap into that source of your power, that's holding out plenty for you.

You are such a beautiful creation, and there really is nothing you should fear!

Each piece of fruit you pluck and eat will bring different gifts your way, you will finally feel joy and happiness.

Chapter 14

Every single one of us is born with a specific state of awareness; some are born with upper levels of awareness; some are born with very low levels. At present most of humanity is currently on the very lower levels of awareness, which in turn corresponds to your vibration.

There are lots of techniques that can be used to measure ones level of awareness, listening is a very good technique, to grow in awareness, you have to step out of your comfort zone, you have to put your way of thinking on the back burner, and listen to the things those with more awareness say, these are usually the people labeled as conspiracy theorists, not all are completely just stark raving bonkers, many things I spoke out about, later on came out as true, you can't judge someone who has really done their research, when you have done none at all.

Would you judge a teacher from teaching you English? No, you wouldn't, and this is no different with a very well researched person. Just because they don't have a degree in their research, it doesn't make a well researched person a conspiracy theorist. This labeling has to stop in order to move forward in a more positive way.

No matter how uncomfortable the truth is to hear, you have to hear it to become more consciously aware. At present most of humanity is on a third dimensional awareness, that needs to change as a collective, meaning together. Most well researched people will also hold a lot of compassion for humanity, so they support you on your journey, your Awakening, because it has to happen, and if it's someone you know, it does make it so much easier, I had that in my friend I spoke of, Michelle West, she helped me through my awakening to the real world, she kept me calm when that pesky fear crept up on me, never once turning me away or ignoring me, and that's why I hold a lot of love & respect to Shelly, my door will forever be open to her, because she didn't turn her back on me, she supported my awakening to the world and how it really works, it was very frightening at first, but you soon learn what are distractions chucked at us to divert our eyes away from the truth! The world literally is a gigantic stage, full of quite evil characters really, these people don't care for humanity, they care for themselves and their own kind of people, they do separate us from them, they see us as hamsters & guinea pigs, nothing more nothing less, these people will never ever dissolve their Egos, because money and status makes them feel superior to us, they do think they are better than us.

So, you have to raise your awareness about the world to bring about positive change.

Seeing isn't believing, believing is seeing! There are great claims surrounding the "Supernatural" psychic abilities, extraterrestrial life, many people want to see the proof!

But what is proof? Proof is defined as the evidence that establishes or helps establish a fact or the truth of a statement. However, is there really such a thing as definitive proof?? If someone you knew was to suddenly be able to disappear & reappear, or even levitate right in front of your eyes would you believe it?

We know there has been and still are great illusionists, Dynamo, who so called walked on water and him, himself levitated, in front of thousands of people, however we know their alleged abilities, they are just illusions to the eye.

We know the great CGI effects Hollywood can come up with, especially disaster movies, they look so real, but you know it's just a film right? Because that's how we have been taught, so how do we know everything covered in the media is fact or proof? We don't, do we really? We have been programmed to believe it, and they were able to continue to manipulate our minds because we are at very low levels of conscious awareness. so, I will ask you again, is there such a thing as definitive proof?? No there really isn't.

But once you accept what is truth and what is utter nonsense, there is no going back and bit by bit as you grow & develop, you will notice more and more things yourself. As your awareness increases, so do all your senses too, you start to become more aware if someone is lying to you, you become more aware if someone is cheating on you.

We noticed this the most as a team, because without knowing we were actually doing it, there has been many a time where we have tapped into each other's consciousness, for example : I had a dream that Our Dawdle was visiting me and every ten minutes she would ask me for cough medicine, well the very next morning our Dawdle had woke up with a very irritating & annoying cough, we were both a little freaked lol, but it happens all the time now, we know when something is wrong with someone else on the team, it's strange to begin with, but it's kind of more exciting than weird now for us, so our levels of consciousness are very high and advanced.

You see how some creators or influencers trick you; they trick you into liking a person that isn't really real, they are playing a role that's all, you don't really know that person, and yet you want to be like them, ask yourself why? Because that lifestyle is portrayed as the best, loads of money, flash cars, big houses, I don't see the good in any of them, all I see is greed and them thinking they are more superior to your average Joe (As they have taught us that phrase.)

It's like for me, I heard a crazy story about the Twin towers disaster, so I decided to look into it myself, and it doesn't make sense how a tiny plane can fly through all that concrete and steel, and to cause the whole building to collapse, if you remember, the second tower going down was announced before it actually happened, how were the media, all the media, in that area at that exact time? How did they know to be there at that time? How did they find a paper passport fully intact and that was how they told the world it was a terrorist attack, I've research that footage, and in all honesty it looks like controlled demolition, for two little planes to cause such destruction when you think it about it logically, it doesn't make any sense at all really! The evil people will do in this world is very very frightening!

It's like the issue with modern science, it only focuses on physical and observed phenomena, and it deems anything that cannot be seen or measured by modern instruments as a pseudo-science.

Nikola Tesla did once say: "The day science begins to study nonphysical phenomena; it will make more progress in one decade than in all previous centuries of existence."

And it has to change, but because as a whole the low level of consciousness and awareness is so low that you believe what they say makes sense, when in fact it doesn't make any sense at all. As your awareness develops more and more and you increase your vibrational frequency, your evidence and your truth will become stronger & stronger, meditation is the key here in aiding you to develop your abilities, work on meditation that stills the mind and lifts the fog, unfortunately you do have to pull back the curtain to see the truth, to deprogram the mind that's been heavily manipulated, it's reaching beyond your comfort zone, it's about being brave enough to break through all you have been taught to believe, and rewire your brain back to it's original state of consciousness, how you entered the world.

This will also help your spiritual awareness, you will be able to work with spirit if you choose, and if you begin to work with spirit, it's important to develop that spiritual awareness through these key points.

1. Close your eyes when you are in a comfortable position.
2. When you are relaxed, imagine you are a tower of white light, shimmering away, connecting you to spirit, connecting you with your higher self.
3. Set an intention in the mind of what you want to know or sense.
4. Move your awareness to your third eye area, focus on that point, because that's where you need to see from.
5. Now feel that awareness in your heart, feel the beat, but listen to the silence between beats, still focusing on seeing through your third eye.
6. Feel all the emotions hitting you, whatever is coming to your mind's eye, feel it all, don't be afraid to let go.
7. Just feel yourself engulfed in white warm light, ask your questions or your intentions.

Feel what your mind's eye is telling or showing you, it's normal to see images, words, numbers, places, try to focus on what these things are trying to tell you. The answers are always inside of you. If you practice this often, even if you don't want to work with spirit, it's a great way to expand and increase your whole awareness, it will aid in raising your vibrational frequency.

It's normal to feel tingling, a little lightheaded, but mostly you normally feel like a blanket of love and warmth has been wrapped around you.

Meditation and connecting with your higher self, is the best way to raise your awareness, increase your vibrational frequency, it does take some getting into as I've said, so will power and determination are really needed, but don't get angry with yourself for not getting it first time or even the tenth time, everyone is different and it does depend on what level of awareness you are already vibrating on. If it's low levels, it will take time. You can't rush this process at all.

It does take pure determination to achieve everything we have spoken of throughout this book, some things are repeated to help you understand better.

Awareness is a very vital important factor of life, way more important than material things, money and status, and you have to think of the effects of you working on yourself, will have a knock-on effect throughout your family, and that's the beauty of this shadow work, surely your family is worth this effort? It doesn't cost you a penny, apart from buying this book, it doesn't cost you a single thing to learn what we have, and to retrain yourself like we have.

I've seen big changes in people after a couple of months, some people really excel in this self-work, you won't ever want your old self back once you have achieved breaking through the Ego and the illusion of the world.

The presence of God exists everywhere and in every single thing, whether it's animals, human beings, plants, objects.

So, for this reason we must understand that all structures are a part of God.

It's part of the collective spirit of the universe.

Structures are also controlled by the laws of the spirit world.

This 3-dimensional world is based upon the laws of the spirit world, which without we cannot exist.

Which means everything and everyone is as much of the eternal Divine Being and alive as anything else in the universe.

It's like you can't have night without day, there always has to be a balance, you can't have Ying without Yang, a balance is always needed, so you have to balance out yourself awareness.

Raise that awareness, learn how to find you, the real you, and don't be afraid to stand alone, like I've said, we are always around for those struggling. Your people will come to you eventually, and you will wonder why you never choose this path sooner, but don't dwell and regret it, you are only human, at least you are doing something to change your future. Some just literally sit waiting for someone else to save them, because they are too lazy to want to put the time and effort into themselves. It's pretty selfish really, especially if you have children and grandchildren, they should be a big enough reason to want to change!

They didn't get a say in whether they wanted to be on this planet or not, you made that decision for them, so it's only right you do something that could end up changing everyone for the better!

Do it with a friend if you don't feel strong enough to do it alone, it will strengthen the bond you have. And support each other through every step, it's not a competition, so don't treat it like one, grow and flourish together, you can even do this with your husband, wife or partner, oh you will notice a huge difference believe us!

This newfound awareness is heavy with responsibility, but it's also a great gift, a chance to connect on a deeper level than you ever thought possible.

A chance to heal, and to rise above the illusion of the world, the Matrix.

CHAPTER 15

If you have gotten this far reading this book, we are proud of you. How do you feel? Did things resonate with you? Are you ready to start your own journey of self-discovery and growth?

Like we said, this book isn't going to be for everyone, and some will probably think it's utter nonsense and rubbish, but we don't care, because it will hit the right people, so opinions don't affect us at all, especially if it's negative, it's our truth, our experiences.

We have already achieved what's in this book, so we don't live in the 3D world the same as you.

None of us would go back to how we were, it's a whole new beautiful and incredible world.

We don't even let what others think of us on TikTok get to us. People believe what they want to believe, and we don't have egos that need feeding, we don't need people telling us we are the best or things like that, we don't want to be the best, we don't want popularity, because this is our passion, we don't use spirit's as performing monkeys as we have stated. We are not knocking anyone in this field, but we are completely different to other paranormal field workers, we are actually doing and creating something, we actually have a purpose, it's why we were all brought together.

We don't believe in coincidence, it's a word, there are no coincidences, everything you go through and get thrown at you, it's by design, what you put out in the universe determines what you get back! And if you are not a nice person at all, you won't ever get treated with love & respect, if you con people and pretend you're something you're not, or you pretend you are doing something for someone, when you're not, eventually it will catch up to you. Karma is very very real, it can take it's time, but it always comes to bite you. So never put out ill intentions on another person, focus and change yourself, if you don't like someone or something, stay away it's that simple!

Why do people feel it's okay to rip into someone on social media? If you don't agree with something, be an adult and scroll past, is there really any need to leave a negative comment on something you don't believe in or even understand? Like recently, we had a negative person who doesn't even know me, call me a con woman lol, and I was to get a proper job, what I do isn't a job, it's the only me time I get, because I'm my daughters full time carer, I had to quit my career 12 years ago! I also don't ask for subscriptions or gifts because I'm not doing this for that, yet this person was saying I was ripping people out of their hard-earned money!

Well obviously I just laughed and commented back being kind, but they continued to say I was a con woman and a fraud. It's people like that who will never achieve breaking through their Ego, their mind is to shut off, they are too frightened of what they can't see, so their instincts are to be a child basically and put negative & nasty comments, they don't know my story, they don't know that some of the team have been and experienced my shed, they knew nothing about us at all (or they did, and sadly their Ego took over) But that's how society has shaped people, and it's just getting worse and worse. You have grown adults spouting about mental health problems, and there they are ripping into someone else, really?? You're an utter hypocrite if you are one of these people, most people do it for sympathy, go live and break down about their mental health problems, then next minute they are shouting at someone, really insulting them, even telling them to kill themselves! You're pretty screwed in the head to do something like that!

I saw one video where a young person held a knife to their throat, and people were being absolutely disgusting telling them to do it. What is wrong with people!! It's so shocking, and what example is that setting for your children? Them hearing you shouting and insulting someone, they will think it's acceptable behavior, when it's absolutely not at all, it doesn't matter who you are, you should never ever tell someone to kill themselves, I understand when it's rapists and murderers, and people who do horrific crimes against other's, but to normal people it's absolutely not okay.

I've been burnt quite badly in the paranormal community; it was never this toxic when we first joined 4 years ago! I tried to help people, some used us for the size of our account, but followers don't mean a thing really, it's the same with likes, what reward do you get or what magic happens when you get 100k likes?? We have given a lot to others, including free protection, free bit's of equipment, all we ever ask if we help someone is to not let anyone else know we helped, because we can't help everyone, that bit was abused by someone, and they were nasty as hell to me, obviously in front of other's, I could of easily defended myself, but I'm just not that person, believe what you want to believe because I just don't care! You do not affect me with toxic words, you are not part of my day-to-day life, so you don't affect me in any way. And if you think we are fake, we don't care, because we know we are true to ourselves, and that's the big difference between us.

People moaning that their content isn't getting the views and likes, but someone who is faking it is? So, this isn't really your passion is it? If you are concerned you are not getting views and likes, you're here for attention, to be noticed, you're lying to yourself by saying it's your passion! We don't worry about likes & views on our clips, I don't put them up for anyone but ourselves and our regular supporters, it's nice to look back on to watch your growth. That's the reason we post highlights, definitely not for likes and views. We are ego free, if someone wants to like, comment, or share your content then they will.

Work on yourselves instead of focusing negativity on others, so what if someone is faking paranormal activity, it's up to people what they believe, who they want to watch, why does it bother you? Only one reason, jealousy & envy because you crave the limelight they are receiving, that's what it all comes down to in the end, keep fooling yourself by saying it's because this is your passion. There are so many scammers on social media, why are you only concerned for the people who fake the paranormal? Why are you not concerned about other people being scammed not through the paranormal? It's surprising what people convince themselves into, it really is.

We just do us now and come off the App, our lives are complicated enough without all the chaos and drama that goes on, we want no part of it. Even as a team we do not talk about others, we talk about our day, our families, but mainly we talk about our growth, encouraging and celebrating every level up, as we call it. I won't ever be used again, people I helped blocked us with no reason, but the real reason is because your scared of what others will think of you, because they are bitching about us in their little clicky tribes they have created.

We don't want that life thanks! We are happy just being us.

A lot of people have approached me over the last 2 years especially, saying they have had a spiritual awakening. My spiritual awakening caused me to pass out at the bottom of my stairs, and when I came to everything felt different, everything looked brighter, and I had this knowledge I didn't have before, which was strange in itself to be honest, and things that would normally have me in bit's, it no longer bothered me, I started to get a real good handle on my emotions, I fully embraced this new side of me which got me off antidepressants and other medications, I saw that what I had always felt as mental health problems, were really not mental health problems, I was an unguided Empath, And when I met my friend who has taught me everything she knows, spiritually. Life started to make sense to me, I didn't look at grief as badly as I did, it gave me strength to let people go, people who were just taking from me, because if they really cared, they would have stuck around to watch me grow. I was able to separate my emotions better, I became a better researcher of the unknown, I was taught how to open my senses, taught how to use the gift inside of me.

I had been looking for something my whole life, and the whole time what I had been searching for had always been inside of me, just waiting to break free, and so that's what I did, I completely let go of that old me and fully embraced the new me, and I've more than made up for the mistakes I made in life, helping others to break free and start living their lives properly is all I want to do, I don't fear failure, it wouldn't even bother me if we only sold ten books, at least I can say I tried to reach out and help people, I put all my life experiences together and used them to help others overcome their fears, failing doesn't make you weak, when you fail you learn a lesson, and life is about learning lessons, good and bad.

You are allowed to grieve for what could of been, you are allowed to grieve for a person you once cared about, you are allowed to grieve that relationship you wish had worked out, surround yourself with people who get you, the real you, the people who don't judge you for what you got wrong in life, or for some action you took because you didn't know any better, it's okay to be triggered by thing's, you shouldn't be made to feel an embarrassment, nobody else has walked your path, nobody else knows the battles you have fought in your own head! If you are getting up every morning, despite feeling broken inside, be proud of yourself. But if you want to change your mindset, you have to be willing to throw everything you have ever been taught to one side, forget about it for now, and focus on finding you!

You deserve to be happy and at peace with who you are supposed to be. Help yourself, you have this book to keep going back to, take your time, slow and steady always wins.

Look at the people you grew inside of you, or who you helped create, you owe it to them to better yourself, set an example for them, you will change their mindset too.

Don't let the fear stop you from playing the game, follow what's inside of you, not what's on the outside, the outside is just a shell, because if I can break through being an alcoholic and breaking through my ego, then I have every faith in you achieving it to.

Say it loud and say it proud! Look in the mirror and love the reflection looking back. Size, weight it shouldn't matter, beauty has always been what's inside a person, we have been programmed wrong! If they had flashed what some call ugly people in programs, singers, influencers etc., 24/7 you would think the pretty people were the ugly ones wouldn't you? Looks has always been used as a weapon, people wanting fake teeth, tummy tucks and boob jobs etc., can't you see it? It's all about money! And that's the saddest truth about life, that it's always been dominated by money and looks, when it really should all be about love, compassion, and kindness.

The human connection has been killed by technology, we need to change it before it is to late, and that change has to start with you. And pay it forward is all we ask, if you achieve what we have, encourage others to do the same, show them the real beauty of life.

Hopefully it will be a domino effect, and remember, it's okay to let go of people, you can still love and care about them, but if they leave you feeling drained, you don't need it in your life.

I have let go of so many people, I had to move forward with my life and start living!

But it doesn't mean I no longer love or care what happens to them, you can't just switch your feelings off, even if it was a one-sided friendship, where you went all in and they didn't, you're still allowed to love & care.

Lean in really, really close and listen. The only thing blocking you is you, remove the blockage, you need to release the emotions of your failures today. Don't hold back tears, anger or frustration, or any emotion that floods you and causes this blockage.

Clear your heart of all the pain and fly above the fears that hold you back. Fear can be crippling for many! But you will rise above your fears, release everything onto your angels, we all have them to guide us through life, you just have to ask for their guidance when you have broken through. And in order to stop letting money be your ruler, you have to admit you have been hurt by it, we all have, because when you pretend the hurt isn't there, it creates barriers between your answers and you! Remember that.

It's okay to feel frightened starting this journey of self-discovery, it will soon disappear, we believe in you! And we believe you can soon be living a much more enjoyable life like you deserve.

Know your worth, and don't just settle, there is a whole new you just waiting to break free, go rescue the younger you, be that support they needed and move forward with no regrets and don't ever, ever look back! Your journey, your life starts today. So, smile and know everything will be okay.

We are alive at this time, we choose to be alive in this part of time, history, this is where the Earth and collective consciousness are being hugely transformed. All the challenges and struggles we are all seeing, feeling, and observing, are the old paradigm energies beginning to shift. You have to be kind to yourself and kind to others. Love always beats the darkness, it lights the path forward, you are so much more than your physical body, so much more.

And at the core of you, there is incredible love, peace and happiness, and when you return to who you were supposed to be, you empower the rise of love within you, and all around you which empowers the shift, and empowers the light of spirit, higher consciousness means more blessings. Returning to love isn't easy, it's the biggest challenge of all. But you can overcome this, so you powerfully shift out of your old patterns, and fully embrace the new.

This is a powerful life journey, so write it down, keep a journal, you may tweak our teachings, and your ways may help others someday!

Take a leap of faith for YOU. Because you are worth it.

Chapter 16

About Somerset Paranormal Tales

We don't like to put ourselves in the section of paranormal investigators as, we prefer researchers, because that's what we really are!

We are not here to prove life after death exists, it's our belief it does, we want to understand it, know what it is, where we go, we have so many questions!!

We literally opened up a right can of worms, but we've had quite a few questions answered, like some spirit's can read the chat, they can read messages I type out and give a response if it's correct, it's pretty mind blowing, they can even answer with me asking questions in my head!

Every time we do a session, we are learning, we log everything on a session, every word, name, we log everything and the answers we get to questions, we have proven theories, and we are embarking on a little team experiment very soon, we are all excited to see if we can achieve it, although it may take a few attempts, we will keep trying, and I do hold out hope that we will achieve it.

I was taught how to read spirit energy by a brilliant lady, but what I didn't know until I met her, was that I carried that gift inside of me, I just always felt I didn't belong here, I didn't fit, and this lady changed my whole life.

So, we focus on asking the same kind of questions to different spirit's, we are also able to help lost, trapped, and confused spirit's! Some don't even know what's happened to them, so as well as learning, we also give back by helping!

It took some learning, but I was taught how to open a portal of light to help spirit pass over, and sometimes I feel the spirit pass through me, one time a young girl passed through me and I felt all her pain, I saw her life, I felt her death, it was a very overwhelming feeling and I did cry.

We have files on lots of spirit's we have helped and our regular visitors. We are given information and insights into future events and disasters.

We are fully connected back to our spiritual side, and that isn't sitting on the floor cross legged meditating, we hold fear for nothing! It's a whole new level of freedom that we want others to experience.

We do get personal messages at times, but we never like people to give us information, we prefer to hear the information from spirit and what Ali reads from the energy, we spent 2 solid years building up a great connection to the spirit realm, or realms. But we cannot guarantee a message would come through, Ali would love nothing more than to be able to control what spirit comes through, but sadly she can't, and again if she could, she wouldn't charge people, because Ali is not driven by money or popularity! She wears her heart on her sleeve.

We want people to learn along with us, but you really do have to have an open mind to help you best understand.

What areas of your life or current situations are coming under the microscope?

The opportunity is here to reflect and observe where you are, who you are.

Where you are heading and what changes need to be made to bring both of these areas into alignment with your highest intentions and values. Change is a word that most people fear or are frightened of, but remember, change is a key part of positively aligning with a higher level of your unique, authentic, and most vibrantly beautiful self.

Connecting with your higher self has never been needed, you need to navigate through the clutter and illusion into a newfound clarity and progress on the highest possible path for your life.

And make sure you take the time to stop, step back and observe, and allow yourself to tune into underlying blessings in each and every moment of your journey.

So that's us! We are all very proud Empaths that are blessed with different gifts and are warriors of the light. We know if people are lying or playing us now! We have all grown a lot in the last 6 months, especially me as a person! We have been taught some tough lessons and many of us have been through some real traumas. However, we help each other to grow and shine and we don't talk about others or get involved with drama or gossip. We literally do us. We stay in our lane and don't swerve. It's not that we think we are better than anyone else. We don't assume to be the best team and in fact we don't want to be the best. We don't seek fame or fortune. In fact, we couldn't think of anything worse. If we had, we would have got it by now - especially with some of the stuff that's happened and our communication with the spirit realms. Someone kindly called the media on our behalf, and they seemed very surprised when I turned them away. I have turned down a private investor. I don't feel that we should ever be owned or controlled.

So why this book? In truth, we just don't have the time to do one on one or group sessions. We all have our individual lives to live, some of us pretty difficult ones, but we wanted to help others. So, the idea was that we would write it all down and try and help others. It's all here in the book for you to keep going back to. All I and the team have ever wanted - is to help.

Our whole focus is on finding answers and discovering who we truly are. As a team, we have a very close connection. We are more like a family really. We inspire and encourage one another. Cheering each other on. Sailing through the highs and getting through the lows together. Although I think I'm finally done with my low days, apart from when I push myself too hard during a session. If there is someone wanting to reach out, I give my all into maintaining that connection and helping them to get answers. However, until we know what the message is it can still burn me out. In the end it's worth it to get a message to someone who has desperately been wanting to hear from a loved one.

I don't ever open a session expecting some message for myself, I've never done that. But I did have a couple of messages. One in particular gave me closure and it was like a weight had lifted off my shoulders, after carrying it all these years. I asked specific questions from spirit to be sure I was talking to who they said they were, and each answer just blew me away.

But I would rather have messages for those desperate to hear from someone. All of us on the team feel the same way, as much as we feel so blessed to hear from people we love or loved. We would prefer our supporters get their messages and never think of ourselves first - not ever.

We recently had a message for a very lovely loyal supporter, and I know secretly she had been wanting to hear from this loved one. I remember getting overwhelmed and having to pause the live. I recomposed myself and managed to stay focused and keep the connection open. I was so happy to have been able to give her that gift, and her loved one certainly put on a show especially for her, it was amazing. The whole team felt that live and that connection because that's how connected we are as a team.

CHAPTER 17

Teams Personal Entries

Our Dawdle; I was scrolling through TikTok one afternoon, my daughter had just introduced it to me. When I came across something that was strange to me. In a churchyard sat two little white teddies and a box with flashing lights (which I later learned was a K2) and the lovely soft voice of a lady. I was simply mesmerized by what I was seeing. I have always been interested in the paranormal and have had a few experiences myself. This though, was something totally different to anything I have ever seen before. I continued to watch these lives and before long I was asked to be a moderator. I have been with Ali ever since. I never thought I would witness what I have during this time, and it has truly been an awesome journey so far.

As a Reiki Master, I have always been quite spiritual, knowing about energies and chakras, and the flow of energy through the body, but Ali has helped me hone my skills, further by teaching me about spirit guides and how to find out who mine are and how to connect to them.

Being a part of Ali's team and sharing her journey has been amazing and I still have a lot to learn, I am a totally different person to who I was before I found SPT but with Ali's guidance I know I shall become the best person I can possibly be.

Baz: I've always had a belief in the paranormal and had some form of gift/ ability to sense certain things. Within my current time with Somerset paranormal Tales, I've become far more aware of a lot of things. Witnessed things I never expected to and gained much knowledge & understanding.

And seen, not just myself but other team members grow and change over time, I've been surprised by some too!

This journey has proven that we are learning each and every day, everyone should be proud of themselves! It's a whole new exciting world out there, and we are very happy our paths crossed. Learning from Ali has changed our lives, and we have never been happier. You don't have to unlock that spiritual part if you don't want to, but it is a whole new world, we are glad we took that leap of faith. The work isn't difficult to do on yourself, it's exciting and a whole new feeling. You won't regret it!

Tash (Tick Tack): I have always believed there is life after death, I have however had my eyes (all three) opened even more since joining Ali's team. Not just from the amazing activity the shed gives us, but from my own personal spiritual journey and learning from everyone on the team how to open and connect with spirit.

I have discovered who one of my spirit guides is (with the help of the team) and his name is Walter. Now Walter has made himself very very comfortable in Ali's shed and helps her out when needed, argues with her and he's also partial to laughing at her, which is hilarious in itself. I have given Ali another resident spirit who goes by the name of Chief, real name Scott, and he really loves to wind Ali up on a daily basis! Sorry not sorry lol.

I personally have changed so much since finding Ali and the team. At the start of this amazing journey I was really struggling with my moods and ended up going on antidepressants, which did help a little bit, I actually thought I was an emotion less robot, but I slowly began to learn about myself on a deeper level, having the support of some very special people and how the moon actually affected me! I wasn't being moody as I now call it, I was feeling 'Moony' lol, I didn't realise, one I was an Empath, and two, being an Empath can explain 'Mood shifts' so long story short I am now not on any sort of antidepressants and living my BEST life!

I have recently discovered I can hear spirit and very very recently discovered I can also see spirit! Which is absolutely amazing!

I could go on for pages, but I won't lol, I am so very grateful for everyone on the team with all their help, support, advice, and laughs / GIF wars we have.

It's a whole new beautiful world and I wouldn't go back to the old way of living, not ever!!

Jess: Hey I'm Jess / Fox

Going back to the start of my life, I was always called "an old soul" I believe an old soul is somebody that has had either one or more past lives. I have memories of being in my pushchair and walking around a town I'd apparently never been to before, telling my mum things like "in my old life, when I was a boy called Tom, the butcher's used to be on this street!" Apparently as a baby I'd babble and chatter to things in the room. When I could finally start saying words I'd freak my mum right out by telling her there was a man stood in the room and point.

Growing up, I'd always have night terrors well into my teens. They were always so vivid, and I'd be visited by spirit's every evening. I was scared, really scared to my core because I didn't know what was happening. I'd be laid in my bed for hours trying not to fall asleep because I didn't want the ghosts to come back! When I couldn't fight the sleep anymore and was just about to drift off, I'd hear this static radio noise that sounded like muffled talking in the distance. I would go around and check the house in case mum or dad had left the tv/radio on downstairs but the whole house would be dark and nothing on, with everyone asleep in their beds...I was so confused! I had no idea Why I was hearing the talking or what it was, but it would happen just before I fell asleep every night. Then came the faces along with the talking. When I'd close my eyes I'd hear the muffled talking alongside people's faces coming into my mind's eye. As a child I had absolutely no idea what was going on so I just put it down to "This must be 'normal' everyone gets this." I Remember asking my brother and sister if they hear what I did, and they looked at me like I was mad! It was from that moment onwards; I knew I was different.

It wasn't until my teenage year's I realised not everyone can absorb other's emotions and "put yourself in their shoes" (I know now, this is because I am an Empath) I didn't find it hard at all to understand how someone was feeling without them telling me - it was their energy.

I'd be coming home from school exhausted, because being around teenagers all day every day, with lots of different emotions, dramas, and other stuff, was draining me, as an Empath.

When I got to my early twenties, I was quite heavily into social media and found myself enjoying the pagan Instagram pages. I could relate to everything that paganism had to offer, and I went on an upward spiral from there really! This is when I researched and researched! I LOVED the old ways, the witchy ways, the natural ways. There was Wiccan, Neopaganism, druids, ALL SORTS! I felt like I'd found my people. The natural healers, the tarot card readers, they are all amazing.

It was around this point I realised that perhaps I wasn't just an Empath but also psychic because I was realizing I was an Empath with a little added spice. There was something a little different with me than the other Empaths I knew. So, I went to my local psychic medium that was offering classes. It only took me one class to realise that I do, in - fact have the gift. I then bought my first Oracle cards and never looked back!

I believe that the universe bought me to Somerset Paranormal Tales for a reason and I needed a spiritual family to enable me to grow and fulfill some sort of higher calling. I'd always liked the paranormal, but the way Ali was conducting her lives, was different. She wanted answers, not the scare factor. She was thinking from the same perspective as myself and shows so much respect for spirit's. This is the reason I kept coming back into her live every night. I could feel it wasn't your average 'Paranormal investigation' there was something more to it.

Since I was asked to join SPT as a moderator, I finally found my spiritual family. I can talk to them about anything and everything and I know because we have shredded our Ego's there is no judgement, no selfishness only love and uplifting between us all and for that, I thank you all so much. I know we've all been put in this team for a reason. Light workers unite!

Ali has been like a mentor for me. Although she is still learning as well, she's able to use what she's learnt to teach me & the guys. The amount of knowledge she has is just insane!! Ali, I'm forever thankful to you for your guidance and support. We keep each other's vibrations high.

I still need to find my calling spiritually. I no longer do paid psychic readings. It didn't feed right taking money from people when I was comforting people, I did not like the pressure of it all. If a spirit comes to me naturally, I will of course proceed. Which I do because they may have an important message to pass on. I do card readings for people when I feel drawn to doing it for them. Perhaps they are going through a hard time and need some guidance, that sort of thing. I do a lot of astral planing and receive messages through dreams. I have started having premonitions recently as well. I suppose only time will tell what the future holds, but for now, I will continue learning as much as I can with the team and their guidance, and support and using Ali's methods to continue my spiritual journey. Never looking back now!

Jo: Hi everyone, well to say I love SPT is an understatement! I've never felt like I belonged anywhere in this world, constantly unsure of who I was, what my purpose was, losing friendships, constantly trusting the wrong people, which led me to believe that I was the problem. One day I randomly stumbled across Somerset Paranormal Tales doing an investigation, I've always had an interest in the paranormal and always drawn to it. Ali and the team from day one, have made me feel so welcome to the point where I view them as family. Not only do I now feel like I belong, but I feel safe, I know my place, I know my destiny. Ali has helped me see my potential and unlock a whole side of me that I never knew was possible, I still have a long way to go, but because of the love, support, and guidance, I know I will reach my full potential in no time. Anything is possible, all you have to do is believe, believe in yourself, find you, break free, and trust the right people, which is what I did. I will be forever grateful to Ali and the team for excepting and loving me.

Kieran: So before I met Ali, I was on my path to finding peace, but really struggling as I had not long come out of a bad/ Abusive relationship, so I was in a lot of heat, with pretty much everything, my anxiety was 10× worse, although I still get nervous around others, but I am more relaxed than I've ever been in my life!

So, 2022 I believe it was when I found Ali, I must admit because I had seen others, that were demanding and being disrespectful to the paranormal, I did judge far too quickly, I soon realised I was very wrong!

I saw how genuine and pure Ali was with spirit's, after hearing more of Ali's story, of how losing her son set her on a path to find answers, I realised how similar we were with one another, and I just fell in love with the team (Ready for my adoption letters) I would say 6/8 months was when I started to feel at peace with people, and within myself to. And within our research it's made me feel amazing! I've never felt so happy and filled with love, in a way I feel like a more reborn, newer more connected version of myself, it's incredible to find peace! I adore all of the team, as well as those who support us.

This bond we share, from our inner roots, it's safe, it's judgment free, it's family. Blood doesn't make you family, it makes you related, love is what makes you family! Love, support, guidance, it's what it's all about. I haven't hit my full potential yet! But with Ali and the team guiding me, I know I will.

Trust that this works, it's not difficult, and we are live every night as a support network, all our inboxes are open, we don't want to be number one, we just want to help people become more free and at peace with themselves. There is no greater feeling than self-love, raising your awareness to what's really around us, technology is like a drug, you can't go without it for a day. When you find yourself and you are at peace with who you are, social media doesn't become addictive, this process changes your whole mindset and awareness, so embrace the power you hold inside. Choose love not material things, choose love and not popularity, find your peace.

Jackie: I came across SPT in 2023, by way of my daughter, who at that time, watched many ghost investigation groups on social media. I was intrigued & watched a few of the groups which she shared with me. I have always had a strong belief there is more to life, other than the illusion that we believe is life...Growing up, living a 9 - 5 job, getting married, having a family, growing old & then you die! I believed that death, was not the end for us & that we are capable of so much more.

I'd attend a local spiritualist church, attend workshops and healing sessions at the church in order to learn more about the afterlife & to grow spiritually. Inevitably, as it does 'life' got in the way for me - I forgot about my beliefs, looking back now, I guess I lost my way and was spiritually numb.

The moment I started watching Ali in her shed was the day I started to get back on track. My passion for the spiritual world was rekindled. The energy & confirmation of spirit I witnessed and still do to this day, is jaw dropping. I am still blown away by what I see, hear & feel...plus I have had the pleasure of meeting Ali & experiencing her shed.

Along my journey with SPT, spiritually & emotionally I started to heal. With their love, support, guidance and understanding, I have been able to build up my self-confidence & begin to wake up.

From reading a book that Ali has written, to books she has recommended, I now know who I am & why I do what I do sometimes and why I behave in the way I do sometimes. I have learned it's because I am ME. That I have a powerful & strong soul.

Unlike the other paranormal teams, SPT have immense respect & trust in spirit and vice versa, which I believe is why there is so much energy in the shed. The connection with spirit goes from strength to strength each time contact is made. For me personally, I owe a great deal of gratitude to the whole of the team, for showing, guiding, and giving me the confidence to believe in myself & my spiritual path. I am truly blessed to be a part of Somerset Paranormal Tales.

Gaz: I have only joined the team recently and it is absolutely blowing my mind. My eyes have been opened to so many things in life which never used to make sense to me. With Ali's guidance and support I feel myself growing every single day. The team as a whole are out of this world. Ever fancied a close, strong, and supportive family? Who never judge you, who you can be yourself fully to? That's exactly what they are. I've witnessed things that with a closed mind you would say were tricks but seeing them with my own eyes demonstrates without a shadow of doubt to me that there is more to life than this earthly body we pilot. I'm so incredibly proud to be on this journey and be doing it with such a formidable team.

Donna: After taking some personal time out from the team, it's so great to be back. I kept continuing what Ali had been teaching me and I feel within myself that I have become stronger than I thought possible, my time with SPT has been incredible and I see things that I wouldn't have ever stopped to think about. Ali may seem different, but her heart is immeasurable, and she literally goes to great length for people she care about. Her heart is rare, she inspires us to reach higher, her support and her strengths are something I've never seen before in anyone, joining SPT was the greatest decision I ever made!

So, you have heard from the team, you have heard how their lives have changed for the better!

Now are you ready or brave enough to find YOU? Do you want to stay stuck just existing, with the occasional holiday or celebration that makes you feel great, then it's back to the dull normal day-to-day things, work, looking after kids, whatever it is you do each day, are you not fed up with it? Do you want a life where every day you wake up and you feel excited for the day ahead? To learn and to grow, to be loved and seen.

It's a rollercoaster to start with, as change is never easy! But change has to come from within, nobody is going to make your life easier or better, only you hold the power to do that. You! Don't waste this amazing human experience, live it, go out on a high with no regrets or unfinished business.

It's not too late no matter how old you are. I'm 49 years old and feel I have wasted most of my years on the wrong things. But if we can help others to not waste their years away, then it was well worth me wasting mine and I'm happy with that!

We will stay true to who we have become and continue to be that safe space for like-minded souls. You are never alone with us around, as long as you haven't hurt us, we will always be here, true and with our humanity firmly intact! Love, light and positivity always.

We are live every night on TikTok as a support network, or if you do know me then message me, I will do my best to keep you supported, it's easier with a couple of you, much easier. We are just here until you find your people, and even your forever family.

Invest in <u>you</u> for once!

Anyone who may be a paranormal investigator, please check out Pk paranormal equipment only on eBay. Honestly, I have Paul's whole range and it's all amazing! And he isn't in it for the money either, so all of his stuff is affordable and under £100. He does an amazing motion activated music box for less than £70.

The cheapest one I've seen that's decent, not a handmade wooden box either, is £140 so Paul is half that price and some. His writing is in green so just type in eBay P K paranormal, and you will find him.

If anyone is looking for a freelance designer then please contact our designer Bryn. A truly incredible, talented young woman, who I am so proud to call my friend and a big part of SPT now. I've known Bryn for a while now and she really is the sweetest, kindest person. She really deserves everything so please do think of her if you know anyone looking for a designer. You won't be disappointed at all, she is brilliant!

We have a lot of proven theories about the paranormal, with all the information we have been collecting! But maybe that's a story for another day. Who knows what the future holds for any of us, but I do know one thing, we are all very excited for the future.

We wish you every success in your journey of self-discovery, and remember we are always around if needed. We believe in you, and we are proud of you for buying this and investing in you!

And if you think it's just rubbish, that's your entitlement to that opinion, we don't get offended with having no Ego's, you continue your boring life, because after all "If you can't laugh, you're boring" with Ali a spade is a spade and we wouldn't change a thing about her or anything about us! We are just us.

Love all the SPT crew. xx

Ali Hurd

CHAPTER 18

Forever Our Kathleen

I still can't believe I'm writing this...One special team member I left out was our beautiful Kathleen, she passed in September 2023 and our world was shattered when we lost her, nobody can really understand the bond we all had, we were all strangers on the internet at first, but the connection between all of us is just something I didn't ever think was possible, it's like we had known each other forever, we all just clicked, and the love & respect we felt for one another is something else! She was the most funniest, brilliant, amazing person!! And I would give anything to hear one of your rants again, because they were the absolute best and you would have us in fit's of laughter, that's what we mainly did, laugh, laugh till our bellies hurt, and her smile lit up the room. Kathleen loved us for us, and I bonded with her over the loss of my son, my world fell apart when I lost him,10+ hrs of labour, knowing I wouldn't be taking him home, that bump I had sung to for months, pictured giving him the best life I could, catching his foot or hand when he moved, buying clothes and proudly folding them into a draw. Everyone forgot him, never spoken about again, it was like I couldn't talk about him, it had to be forgotten, and that was torture for me, I had to deal silently alone!! Kathleen understood all of it, and finally someone listened to me! I will always hold such love and respect for Kathleen because she found me, all because of her, I found peace within myself, and I absolutely hate that she's not here with us! My heart also aches for Kathleens family! Having a mum like her must of been incredible, she loved her children and grandchildren with every inch of her heart, always talking about her grandchildren and you could literally feel her love for her family just flooding out of her, to loose someone so incredibl well the pain, the huge hole left in your heart, the ache...That's the worst thin about being a true Empath, is you literally feel everyone's pain & hurt, w absorb it (which I will explain in the next chapter) But I also knew, once she ha grieved her passing, she would give signs, I know she will always be watchin over her family, and I know they will always feel a painful ache in their hear because she should still be here, and I did get angry at the spirit realm for moment, thinking we had been helping, so why couldn't they have warne us or saved her, but I know it doesn't work that way sadly! But we will foreve carry her in our hearts, and keep her memory alive, until our time comes, an we meet again! I focused on being the strong one for the team, and I guess pretended she was still here, so it wasn't until this year that my grief hit and hit hard, she helped me so much and loved me for me, faults, scars and all, sh loved me the way I was, so I can't let her down and just stop doing this, we hav always wanted to help others, she would kick my back side if I didr continue with this. And I made a promise to her that I would never chang who I had become.

And I won't ever break my promise to her because I know it would devasta her and I would be in serious trouble when my time comes. I never thought would miss someone so much, she just always had the right things to say, hurts that I can't just call her, I miss seeing a GIF from her when I come c live, it's all the little touching things you miss, and even though her wor was ripped apart, Kathleens daughter told me how much her mum loved m even made sure Kathleen was wearing her team bracelet, only because i kne she panicked when she didn't have it on, so I just found it comforting Kathleens daughter certainly carries all of her mums qualities, and i know ho proud Kathleen was of her children...we are still connected through our bracelet and I can't thank Kathleen daughter enough for doing that for us, especial when her heart was literally shattered into a million pieces. She's a real credit t her mum, and she has her mum's strength, she may not believe she doe: but she does, and I know Kathleen will always be checking in on her famil Standing proud as she always did, talking about her family! God we all mis you so much, so so much. Nothing can ever match up to you, still can't brin myself to unmod you either, and in all honesty, I don't think I ever will be ready to do it.

And we know full well those bottles will fly one day, they were her favourite. How she would rip into me when they got knocked over and I couldn't stand them back up, she would be in fit's at me having a go at myself, because I'm always telling myself off doing some sort of commentary on what I'm doing, I think that's what Kathleen loved most about me, that I was me and I didn't care what anyone else thought of me, don't like me, don't watch it's that simple! And that I had no shame or fear, sometimes I can act a little crazy, but if it makes someone smile, that's all that matters, and I sure did make Kathleen smile, I'm tearing up just thinking back over those times, why you, we should of had years together, we should be having adventures together it absolutely sucks!!!

I hold her last words to me in my heart always, I was going through a tough time, and something had happened, and after I ended the live that night, I had a message from her with a load of I love you Gif's and this message;

"You carried yourself well tonight love, I'm so proud of you, love you."

I hope we are making you proud, and thank you for being a part of my life, even though it wasn't as long as we had planned, and I know it was you're doing, that I connected with my son, I feel whole again because of you my beautiful Kathleen, even though my heart hurts missing you! I know you did that for me.

"Our Amazing sister Kathleen, in the short time we had you with us, you bought joy, love and laughter to us all, you made us laugh on team calls, you are missed greatly.
until we meet again Love Baz xxx

Ali Hurd

My darling Kathleen,
Your laugh, your smile, your rants, and your love,
that's what I miss now that you've gone above.
Our long chats and fun I miss every day.
It's not been the same since you went away.
So, I light a candle for you and our team.
We could never replace our Beautiful Kathleen!
Love you always my Angel.
Love your Dawdle xxx

Kathleen – It's Not Goodbye
It's not really goodbye, is it my dear?
Because goodbye is too final,
It's something we fear.

Now here's the part where you come in,
My lovely friend,
I know you're not gone forever,
This is not the end.

I see the signs you send me,
The little robin and butterfly too,
They say it's divine timing,
You do it right on cue.

I miss you every day,
But then I'll hear a song or rhyme,
That makes me think of you,
And I know you're doing fine.

I'm not going to write what I miss about you,
Because in reality you're still here,
Making those teddies flash,
And we know you are near.

As I make plans to visit Somerset,
Anticipation in my head,

Ali Hurd

I hope to hear those Rem Pods beep,
I'll see you in the shed.

A poem for Kathleen by Jessica (Fox)

When I first started watching in 2022, I came on thinking, here we go another staged set-up, but shortly seen within one week I was wrong! I grew a liking to Ali, and more curiosity to the spirit world, I always knew it was real, but I was blinded by fear, so ignored certain stuff, but within the first year I grew a lot more free, less scared of everything, and felt like I was finally living life.

After lots of calls, I would watch everyone and see their beautiful shine, especially our beautiful Kathleen, she was so welcoming and just a rare woman, who I will love forever, I always saw her as a big sister, I miss her daily! Until we meet in our SPT mansion. All my love Kieran xxx

We never had the honor of knowing you, but the stories we've heard from the guys, and the love you left behind, we wish we had, because you sounded so amazing! We will look after the guys for you, and make sure our team reaches the end of its journey! Rest in peace Kathleen #SPTheartbeat Love Tash & Jackie xxx

Our beautiful Kathleen, how I miss that smile that could light up a whole room, I miss you so very much, and it doesn't seem fair that you're not here with us, there isn't a day go by where I don't think of you, so selfless and loving, the lump in my throat I get, knowing you won't be on the next family call, it hurts, I will always treasure the time we did get with you. Love you always princess. Love you always Jo xxx

Kathleen had a heart of gold, and she always checked on everyone and always made you smile. Kathleen was kind, caring and I miss her so much, but know Kathleen will always be with us. Love Donna xxx

I haven't been on the team long but being Jo's partner, I heard all about how amazing she was, I only wish I had the honor to actually meet her, but promise I will look after them all for you Kathleen. Love Gaz xxx

Kathleen touched the life of many, she changed us as people, with her love and understanding. We hope we are making you proud. We will always carry you in our hearts. And we won't ever, ever let you be forgotten, we owe you that much, so sleep tight our beautiful angel, and goodbye for now, we know we will hear from you when you are ready!

Until that day comes, we will continue to just be us, just like you always told us to be. And Ali will continue to knock stuff over, hoping you are watching so you can have a chuckle, we miss you so very much!!

After reading this book I hope you realise your worth and how important self-love and self-respect is. It is not selfish to want to find peace in who you really are as a person, not what society, and everything else has made you think you are.

Never be anything but YOURSELF and don't worry you will find your people. This team is living proof of that. You were born to live not exist, so live, truly live.

We are always live in the evenings to be a support network. This is serious work on you and it's not going to be easy so don't hesitate to reach out and always remember the past is just that. You can't change it. You have no control over it, but you do have control over your future. Make it count and leave this life with no regrets.

Ali Hurd

Events

Airbase

Somerset Paranormal Tales investigation events in the local area - give full protection everything safely, no risks taken.

Printed in Great Britain
by Amazon